ETHEL WATERS

I TOUCHED A SPARROW

ETHEL WATERS

I TOUCHED A SPARROW

SPECIAL CRUSADE EDITION

Published for the

Billy Graham Evangelistic Association

Published by

World Wide Publications

1303 Hennepin Avenue
Minneapolis, Minnesota 55403

ISBN 0-8499-0084-0
Library of Congress catalog card number: 78-51889
Printed in the United States of America

Some of Ethel Waters's statements and reminiscences are from the record Just a Little Talk with Ethel, © 1977 Word, Incorporated.

The quotations in chapter 2 from His Eye Is on the Sparrow, by Ethel Waters with Charles Samuels (New York: Doubleday & Company, 1951), are from pages 201, 248, 249-50, 277-78.

The quotations in chapters 2 and 5 from To Me It's Wonderful by Ethel Waters (New York: Harper & Row, 1972), are from pages 9-10, 153.

The hymn "His Eye Is on the Sparrow" is by Mrs. C. D. Martin (1906).

The song "Stormy Weather," by Ted Koehler and Harold Arlen is copyright © 1933 by Mill Music, Inc. Copyright renewed, assigned to Arko Music Corporation. Used by permission.

The song "I Could Never Outlove the Lord," copyright 1972 by William J. Gaither, is used by permission.

The quotation from "Remembering Ethel Waters" by Leonard Feather, Los Angeles Times, Sept. 3, 1977, is copyright, 1977, Los Angeles Times, and reprinted by permission.

Grateful acknowledgment is made to Paul Harvey for permission to use his description of Ethel Waters's performance; and to the following for permission to quote their letters to Ethel Waters: George Burns, Scott Ellis, Bob Hope, Art Linkletter, Mrs. Jack Parker, Corrie ten Boom.

Introduction

Ruth Bell Graham

Getting to know Ethel Waters was one of the most enriching, merriest, most educating experiences of my life.

Seldom does one have the opportunity to meet, much less get to know, a living legend. And Ethel Waters was just that.

Before I had ever met her, I had read "His Eye is On the Sparrow" and been haunted by it.

Later this Sparrow landed in the choir at the first Madison Square Garden meeting. Quite a substantial sparrow whose only request was that she might be allowed to sing with the choir. By removing an arm rest, she comfortably filled two seats. And never missed a night.

From then on Ethel Waters' life took on a new dimension: from entertainment to ministry. To know her life's story is to understand why she loved her Saviour (whom she referred to as "my precious Jesus") so much.

That love spilled over to the Team. She had no family and looked on the Team as her family. She was like a mother to us and we were her children.

And her love overflowed to every audience, and through TV to millions more.

If God could reach down and pick up an unwanted, illegitimate girl and keep His eye on her, guiding her through tragedy and triumph till one day He could use her to tell millions of His great love, is anybody hopeless?

Preface

ETHEL WATERS HAD TAKEN New York by storm long before I was born in an Iowa blizzard.

She had already received wide acclaim in elite nightclubs singing such hits as "St. Louis Blues," "Dinah," "Taking a Chance on Love," and "Stormy Weather," when she became the first Negro woman to star in a Broadway play.

The street life Ethel learned as a child in the slums of Philadelphia and Chester, Pennsylvania, contrasted greatly with the sheltered life I lived in the protective care of my parents in Correctionville, Iowa (pop. 992—all white). I didn't know what a ghetto was. I never met a colored person until after I was eighteen. *Racial prejudice* were words unknown in my vocabulary.

By the time I boarded the yellow school bus to start kindergarten, Ethel was starring in the Broadway play *The Member of the Wedding,* was being seen in such movies as *Cabin in the Sky* and *Cairo,* and had been nominated for an Oscar for her part in *Pinky.* Even if her films had come to my little town, I would have missed them, since the local rundown movie house was "off limits" to those of us from the evangelical church.

The big event in my life in 1957 was my eighth-grade graduation. I proudly wore the yellow chiffon dress my mother made for me as I took my place in the front row of our gymnasium. I was elated as I walked to center stage to get a big red "C" to wear on my sweater and a pin for my achievements in music. Ethel had a big event that year also —she turned her life over to Jesus. He had already been my friend for more than five years.

After completing my thirteen years at the big brick school house, I left Correctionville to conquer greater things. Traveling three hundred miles to Minneapolis to attend business school was the first battle won.

My wildest dreams could never have envisioned the opportunities in store for me when in 1963 I began working at the Billy Graham Evangelistic Association. My work as secretary to Billy Graham's press representative carried me to crusades in distant cities and countries.

Through my work, God brought me to a beautiful relationship with Ethel Waters. Though we were so far apart in our origins, the twelve years after we met proved to be a happy if bumpy ride, in which I shared her joys, hurts and tears—first as a good friend and then after we both settled in Los Angeles, as her "Girl-Saturday." (Each Saturday I'd take dictation, shop for groceries, and sit with her for long periods of time to help alleviate her loneliness.) I didn't take any salary for working for Ethel, but since she had always "paid her own way," we agreed to her giving me $25 a month for car expenses. That arrangement continued until her death.

Each weekday I would give her a phone call. Ethel had a way of answering the telephone with a "hello" that sounded as though she were at death's door—a sort of low painful groan. (This was done so that someone calling a wrong number would not recognize "the Ethel Waters," or if it were someone she didn't especially care for, it would discourage a long conversation.) When she would recognize my voice on the phone, the sparkle that characterized Ethel Waters would spring back into the conversation that followed.

My work as executive secretary to Bill Brown, president of World Wide Pictures in Burbank, California, did not allow long hours to spend with her during the week so these regular phone calls were my assurance to her that I cared.

One night while I was talking with Mr. Brown and his wife Joan about both the trials and happy adventures of my Saturdays with Ethel, Mr. Brown suggested I write down some of my experiences. "You're probably closer to her than anybody," he told me. "God has given you a unique opportunity to touch one of His choicest sparrows."

Not one sparrow can fall to the ground without your Father knowing it.

Jesus said that!

"Now my life is reflected in the songs I sing about God's love. If I get a heart attack, I'm not going to call on 'Stormy Weather,' I'm going to call on my Jesus."

Chapter One

OCTOBER 31 WAS ONE OF THOSE rare smogless Southern California days—the clear sky revealed the majestic mountains of the San Gabriel Valley. It would have been nice to spend this Sunday afternoon basking in the glorious sunshine.

But it was Ethel Waters's birthday, and I wouldn't have missed her special day for anything. I knew "Mom," as she liked me to call her, was experiencing "stormy weather" with her health. Bill and Joan Brown and I planned to spend the afternoon with Ethel.

Halloween day, 1976, was the milestone of Ethel's eightieth birthday, and she was alone in a tiny private room in the hospital. For over five weeks now she had been receiving daily radiation treatments for cancer. Her suffering was very great, and each time I visited her, it hurt me deeply to see her writhe in pain.

Ethel had known suffering for a long while with her hypertensive heart failure, congestive heart trouble, high blood pressure, ulcers, diabetes which had caused partial blindness, and a tumor referred to by doctors as "the size of a volleyball." Now she awaited the important decision as to whether or not surgery should be considered.

As the Browns and I got out of the car and walked toward

the hospital, we were laden down with bunches of fresh flowers, including ones from singer Doug Oldham, writer Eugenia Price, and a special friend, Fred Dienert. We also carried several packages which had been left with us to take to her. Ethel just wasn't feeling up to having other visitors, so we were the privileged messengers.

The words "City of Hope" marked the entrance to the hospital. We were grateful for this place, one of the nation's most outstanding cancer research centers. But we knew that Ethel was well aware of another "city of hope," one that was not located in Duarte, California, but in a special place prepared by the Savior she had come to love. We had often heard Mom talk about being "homesick for heaven." Once when I was with her in Seattle, she had told a reporter, "I know where I'm going and I've got my bags packed. I'm just waiting for my Heavenly Father to snap the lock when He's ready to call me to my final home."

In the hospital, the strong medicinal smell in the corridor was a sharp contrast to the fresh air outside. Walking down the long hall, I noticed some empty rooms which indicated a number of patients had recently gone home—either to their earthly or their eternal one. I couldn't help but wonder how much longer Ethel would have to be here alone in this institution.

Looking like a walking florist shop, we received smiles as we passed the nurses' station. One or two of the nurses who had been there when I checked Ethel into the hospital greeted me. Room 639—the last one down the corridor—had a huge hand-written sign taped to its door. "Absolutely No Visitors, Including Staff." It seemed Ethel had been constantly bothered by visits from numerous staff members, nurses, and other office personnel from the hospital. It was not every day they had a celebrity as one of their patients. Ethel's private nurse, Mrs. Mickelson, agreed it was time for a sign to be posted on the door when one of the nurses came in to ask

Ethel for her autograph while she was on the toilet!

But we were special, and so we ignored the sign, knocked gently and walked in. Ethel had been expecting us. She smiled faintly through much pain. Even though she had lost so much weight, she was too big to be really comfortable in the twin-size bed. Joan and Bill each took a seat in the corner by the window and I perched myself on the foot of the bed. Ethel lay motionless on her back, her copper-colored skin a sharp contrast to the white sheet pulled over her. Mrs. Mickelson quietly slipped out of the room so we could be alone with her.

Ethel was obviously pleased that so many had remembered her on her special day. The purple orchids and violets (her favorite color) cheered her and brought life into the little room bounded by the stark white walls. Her morning had been a busy one with telephone calls bringing love and greetings from Ruth and Billy Graham, Julie Harris and her dear friend, Mary Crowley, whose concern and generosity was making it possible for Ethel to have Mrs. Mickelson there with her.

I helped her unwrap her packages, saving the gift from the Browns and me until last. We had written to over a hundred celebrities and friends, telling them that Ethel would be in the hospital on her birthday and nothing would please her more than to hear from them. Almost every one of them responded. We had their letters and cards bound into a beautiful book and presented it to her. She was overwhelmed and the tears flowed down her beautiful face.

The first letter Bill Brown read to her was from Frank Sinatra, calling her his favorite sparrow. The warmth of their friendship was evident by his signing the letter with his given name, "Francis Albert."

I had read the letter when it arrived, but to hear it again and see how it touched Mom's heart brought tears to my eyes.

Bill continued to read with a letter from comedian George Burns:

Don't ask me how I found out (I have spies everywhere), but I understand you are soon going to turn 80. Well, kid, I got you beat because I'm coming up 81 on January 20. Why don't we team up and show 'em what show business is all about.

Happy Birthday, Ethel! And many, many more. Hope to hear that you're back to good health real soon. I'm sending out special vibrations in every direction.

With Love.

From Bob Hope:

I hear by the grapevine that you are ready to celebrate your 80th birthday. My fervent hope is that you get out of the hospital very soon so you can entertain as you best know how by using your talent to make people happy.

I get a smile on my heart every time I see your picture in the paper and I know that other people feel the same way.

Again my congratulations.

Warm regards.

Art Linkletter's words pleased her:

I hope this birthday greeting doesn't get lost among the many you will be receiving today! More than anyone in our business you are the most universally admired and respected person I can think of. More, you are the most cared about, and the most loved. When I think of you it is almost as a symbol—except that no symbol can evoke the humaneness and warmth that you have always represented. Still, the world does regard you as a beacon, as a human goal to shoot *for—because you are and have always been that rarest of the species: a great human being, wise in the wisdom of the heart.*

We love you.

Warmest congratulations from an old friend.

Congratulations followed from Los Angeles Mayor Tom Bradley who sent a proclamation citing October 31 as "Ethel Waters Day in L.A.," a telegram from former President Richard M. Nixon, letters from First Lady Betty Ford, Dale Evans, Gene Kelly, Fred Astaire, Ralph Edwards, Carol Channing, a card signed by the members of the Billy Graham Team and letters from a host of others.

For more than a half hour Bill Brown read letters, and for more than a half hour Ethel Waters cried—finding it difficult to absorb all at one time such a large quantity of love from so many friends.

As Bill got ready to read the last letter, one from Corrie ten Boom, the heroine of *The Hiding Place*, I remembered back to the first time Ethel had met Corrie.

Corrie had arrived at Ethel's Los Angeles apartment with her secretary Ellen and Mr. and Mrs. Edgar Elfstrom. Ethel joyously embraced this woman who had suffered so greatly in concentration camp. Here were two women very different, yet very much the same. Two women who through their adversities in life had profoundly learned that Jesus is Victor!

In her print dress and long white hair pulled back into ponytail style, Ethel had taken her usual chair by the window. She began chatting away. Ellen and I were amused each time Ethel called Corrie her "precious baby girl," because we knew that Corrie was five years older!

Ethel had been excited with her special visitor. She dominated the conversation, hardly giving anyone else a chance to speak. When she paused a moment for a breath, Corrie seized the opportunity. She gently reached for Ethel's hand

and quickly but quietly began to pray. She thanked the Lord for the witness and blessing Ethel had been to so many millions through her singing. Following the beautiful prayer, Ethel began to sing softly:

> I sing because I'm happy,
> I sing because I'm free,
> For His eye is on the sparrow
> And I know He watches me.

That tender moment and the impact of the message had affected all of us deeply and we all had to fight back the tears.

I had stayed after the others left the apartment and was surprised when Ethel said to me, "Twila, did I say the right things? I'm really not feeling well. I'm in a lot of pain."

In spite of the pain, Ethel, the trooper that she was, never let it be known to Corrie.

Corrie's letter to Ethel on her eightieth birthday said:

> We are both at the end of the second half of our lives. What joy that we know that the best is yet to be, a permanent house in Heaven, made not by man, but by God (2 Cor. 5:1).
>
> God give you a joyful 80th birthday and may you be very conscious of the presence of Jesus. How He loves you and me.
>
> In Jesus the Victor United.

"They are all so beautiful," Ethel sobbed.

Knowing the activities of the day were almost too much for her, Bill said a prayer and we kissed her good-bye so she could get some rest.

As I opened the door to leave the room, I glanced back at Ethel. Her eyes were still misty. That day she had cried more than I had ever seen her cry. I was grateful they were tears of joy. Joy in her heart for so many friends who loved her and especially for the joy she felt from her "precious Jesus."

I was wrong, though, in thinking of her days of illness as "stormy weather." For through them the sunshine of God's love was able to dispel the cloud of darkness for her.

Years ago Ethel introduced the song, "Stormy Weather."

> *Life is bare,*
> *Gloom and mis'ry ev'rywhere*
> *Stormy weather,*
> *Just can't get my poor self together.*
> *I'm weary all the time, the time....*
> *All I do is pray,*
> *The Lord above will let me walk in the sun once more.*

"When I found Jesus," Ethel once said, "I stopped singing the song 'Stormy Weather,' which I had made world-famous. When I sang that song my life was like that. But it isn't any more. Now my life is reflected in the songs I sing about God's love. If I get a heart attack, I'm not going to call on 'Stormy Weather,' I'm going to call on my Jesus."

"Whoever teaches the fish to swim and the birds to fly taught me to sing. I can't remember having a lesson."

Chapter Two

ETHEL WATERS WAS CONCEIVED at knife point when John Waters, a young mulatto, raped twelve-year-old Louise Anderson.

Hurt and bewildered, the young unwed girl was unable to tell anyone what had happened to her. Her mother worked long hours to support the family. And when her pregnancy became obvious, her church, which was so important to her, excluded her. She suffered ridicule but kept her feelings inside.

Louise was all alone at her Aunt Ida's home in Chester, Pennsylvania, when her baby entered the world at 9:15 A.M., October 31, 1896. The woman next door heard her cry out in pain and came to deliver the bright and alert baby girl Louise named Ethel.

It was only natural for Louise to resent this baby born against her will. Fortunately, the young mother lived to see the product of her tragedy of rape reach stardom. Later she also saw how God used her seemingly worthless sparrow to reach many people for Christ.

Louise's mother, Sally Anderson, took over and actually

raised Ethel, and it was her grandmother Ethel called "Mom." But with Sally working as a live-in housekeeper, Ethel was moved around from one broken-down shanty to another in the slums of Chester and Philadelphia. She never knew a secure and stable home life, learning to sleep and eat when and wherever she could. Sometimes she lived with her aunts; often she was completely on her own. Sometimes her mother would get angry at Sally and show it by taking Ethel to live with her. At various times the only home Ethel's grandmother could afford was in the red-light district.

"Sometimes I'd have to sleep on the steps," she recalled, "because my aunts would forget to leave the key in the door. I'd only have a new pair of shoes to try on in the store. The next day they'd go to the pawn shop."

To make sure Ethel was fed, her grandmother would sew pockets inside her apron and fill these with food scraps from her white employer's table. In between these "meals," Ethel learned to survive by stealing. The prostitutes taught her how. "I used to swipe milk from other people's stoops," she later admitted. She was also adept at going out and shopping with a quarter and coming home with a whole meal! She never knew what it was like not to be hungry. At one period, she would get one meal in the evening at a saloon where the people knew her grandmother. Or she'd walk eight or ten blocks to eat fried fish and potatoes for ten cents.

Ethel adored her mother, in spite of being merely tolerated as a daughter. Louise never cuddled or displayed affection toward the young Ethel. "I never belonged," Ethel said of her childhood. "The tug in here wanted to be with her 'cause she was my mother. I always wanted to break down that thing that I felt—that if I could get to know her and she'd get to know me better, she'd like me. That was the childish thought I had." Later she realized that each time her mother looked at her, Louise remembered the most frightening and embarrassing day of her life.

Materially Ethel was more or less getting by. Emotionally she was starved. "I never had a shoulder to cry on or a lap to sit on," she said. "I never got the affection I so desperately wanted." Not even her grandmother, the one person she loved the most and whom she knew loved her, ever kissed or hugged her. She rationalized this lack of physical demonstration of love as caused by her large size. Even at four and five she was taken for much older, and at eleven the men started to be interested in her. She was tall and big-boned, though slender and attractive. She was eager for people to like her and longed for their attention. When she didn't get understanding, she hid her deep hurts and built up defenses of toughness and an exploding temper.

Toughness and temper were almost necessities in order to get along in the ghettos of Philadelphia, Camden and Chester. Alcohol, dope, sex, violence, death—all were a part of that world as Ethel learned about them all. "I got a pretty good education," she recalls, "because anything went in the alley after dark—and I'm not talking about cats and dogs! That way I got my schooling—you know, the school of life—and I'm still attending!

"I was always intelligent. Usually big children are sorta stymied—their intellect doesn't come with their size. I happened to be a pretty big brilliant child!" She had a tremendous memory—"an elephant memory" she called it—and a great capacity for learning from her experiences. The result was that alcohol and drugs were two things she shied away from all of her life. But she became a street child, a dead-end kid, self-reliant, brash, aggressive and wild. No one could beat up on her or put anything over on her.

"Growing up in the red-light district," Ethel confessed later, "I knew all the answers. You couldn't get out of line with me in a minute that I didn't let you know I knew the score. That protected me. I wasn't shy or demure or naïve. I let them know I knew." She may have looked like a child angel, but "I could cuss like a sailor—and I have to pray about that even now! (I never use the Lord's name in vain, but I have a lot of good substitutes.) When you got me mad enough to blaspheme, I was ready to kill you!" She could hold her own with the big kids in the neighborhood because of her size and her profanity.

However, she never resented or was embarrassed by her upbringing. And she could use it to her advantage, getting sympathy because she was a "bastard"—or being defiant because of it.

Ethel found her first understanding and affection at the age of nine when her grandmother, who was a staunch Catholic, enrolled her in a Catholic school in Philadelphia. In an attempt to shield herself from the rejection and hurt she had come to expect, Ethel had built walls of hate between herself and teachers. In this school she immediately set about to establish her reputation as a menace. But this time her contemptuousness and defiance were met with love, her badness and meanness with patience.

The nuns discovered that she wasn't eating lunch. "I never had lunches to carry because there wasn't that kind of food in my house. I'd raise holy hell because I was too embarrassed to go downstairs for lunch knowing I had nothing." The nuns began to find chores she could do for them so they could reward her with part of their lunch—often the only decent meal she got during the day.

The atmosphere of warmth and friendliness that met her from these servants of the Lord gradually changed her. She began to want to behave herself, and she started searching for a closer relationship with God. As she put it, "That was the beginning of me being tamed down and giving serious thinking to the Lord." She learned to pray and to go to confession, though at first she was afraid that her honesty would shock the priest, because "I wouldn't tell a lie. And I wouldn't cheat on the penance even if it took four hours to do the stations. But I made up my mind I wouldn't do that sin again. It was good psychology."

Unfortunately, school occupied only a short part of each day. When she returned home, nothing had changed. The two aunts she was now living with were alcoholics who yelled at her and even beat her when they were drunk. "There was a battle royal then," Ethel remembered, "because I'd learned, from them and others, how to defend myself. I was a good absorber." Her uncle was a kleptomaniac.

At a Methodist Quarterly Meeting in Chester, a very mature twelve-year-old Ethel, who thought she knew it all, found the only One who loves without reservation. Ethel Waters experienced God. She had gone to the first day of the meeting because of the food. Then the gang she hung out with persuaded her to go to the children's revival. Reluctantly, Ethel agreed. She went forward every evening, but nothing happened. The preacher held the meetings open an additional three nights for the children—particularly for Ethel. On that last night Ethel went forward again to the mourners' bench at the closing invitation. Kneeling on the hard floor she cried out to God, "Lord, I don't know why I'm here. I want to know you. I want something, but I don't know how to find it. If I don't get it tonight, I'll never come back."

That night she "came through." God touched her. Ethel Waters knew she had found a Friend, and the people around her knew that she was changed. She was just radiant when she got up, they told her. She knew God loved her and she wasn't alone.

"He let me know there was something," she recalled. "I wanted to hug it. I didn't feel bad about things that hurt me from my childhood that nobody had a chance to know—how lonely I was, how much I wanted affection. I found I had something I could cling to."

But the world she lived in didn't change, and Ethel found

herself facing the dilemma that all Christians do. That is, being in the world but fighting not to be of the world. And when a girl in that church taunted her and accused her falsely, and then raked her face with her long fingernails, Ethel got so enraged that she walked out and never went back. She couldn't honestly go to church with hate in her heart toward that girl. She began the up-and-down continuum that was to be typical of her life for the next fifty years.

"My heart was heavy. Up until the time I rededicated my life, I always had that heaviness, regardless of my success. I was always saying, 'Lord, I know I've failed you. What can I do to get back?' "

When she was thirteen, Ethel married twenty-three-year-old "Buddy" Purnsley. She was coerced into the marriage by her mother, who simply wanted to get rid of her. Purnsley beat Ethel repeatedly and refused to allow her to see her school friends, in order to keep her from finding out about his unfaithfulness. She was a child agewise, but as she told it, her mind was so "old and raw" that she knew the marriage wouldn't last. Although she had "deep religious scruples" against separating from her husband, she did leave him and began to fend for herself. She found work in hotels and apartment houses as a substitute dishwasher, waitress, and cleaning woman. She was such a hard worker that she embarrassed the permanent help.

When she worked as a substitute chambermaid, she'd finish a room fast, then lock the door, and become an actress in front of the mirror. She would dance and sing and imitate the acts she had seen at the local clubs and theatre. Singing and dancing came naturally. "Whoever teaches the fish to swim and the birds to fly taught me to sing. I can't ever remember having a lesson. I had a body and I knew how to use it, doing the shimmy and the shake."

After a couple of years of "just barely making it" with

hotel jobs, one Halloween, her birthday, she was given a chance to sing at a Philadelphia nightclub. "Best present a girl ever had," she said.

The result was that she was hired as a singer and billed as "Sweet Mama Stringbean." One of the songs she wanted to sing was "The St. Louis Blues." When she found out it was protected, she wrote to jazzman W. C. Handy and got his permission to sing it, thus becoming the first woman ever to do so.

Her first performance of "The St. Louis Blues" was at the Lincoln Theatre in Baltimore, where she was billed with the Hill Sisters. The performance was a success, and the money rained down on the stage after her number.

"But the ten dollars a week that looked so good at first got small a few weeks later when I found out that the two boys who got me the job were getting twenty-five dollars a week to manage me," she later recalled.

Her response was to leave them and go with the two Hill Sisters on their own successful tour. This was Ethel's characteristic way of handling injustice. She never stayed in and took it, but stood up to change what she could, and often left to do better somewhere else. She knew that the people liked her way of singing and dancing, and that she could please them. As her reputation grew, so did the crowds. Her absence from a show proved her point to promoters when they failed to get the anticipated profits. And her presence guaranteed a sellout crowd.

Her reputation, however, didn't grow overnight—it took years of appearing in smaller nightclubs on the East Coast or traveling over the country, often with the black Theatre Owners Booking Association. "I worked from nine to unconscious," she said. "But it was fine. I made enough to give up chambermaiding"—though for a time she kept the promise of a job open in case she didn't make it as a performer.

With her career as a professional entertainer/performer

launched, Ethel didn't forget where she was from. She began sending money home to her family, a practice she continued throughout her career. She later said that helping her family was the great satisfaction she got from show business. It was too late to help her grandmother. Sally Anderson had died of cancer in Ethel's arms the year that Ethel was married to Buddy Purnsley. As she was dying, she asked Ethel to sing her favorite song, "His Eye Is on the Sparrow." But Momweeze, as Ethel called her mother, and her aunts, needed her help.

In Harlem between tours, Ethel found work at some of the popular places of that time—Edmond Johnson's Cellar, the Cotton Club, as well as the Plantation Club where she made her first big hit of "Dinah." (Years later an unknown white singer copied Ethel's rendition of "Dinah" for an audition. The show's director, not remembering the young lady's name, kept calling her Dinah. The singer then took that name as her stage name, and as Dinah Shore she became a favorite of millions.)

Ethel's popularity increased and she began to record her singing, first with Black Swan and then with Columbia Records for nearly ten years. In the early 1930s Ethel was practically the only Negro star vocalist on records. "There was just something about me and my style that the people wanted to hear." She was able to capture and project emotion—any emotion—in her singing, drawing on her own experience and deep feelings.

She was heard on radio each week from the Cotton Club, where she was backed by the Dorsey Brothers' orchestra.

Her first Broadway appearance was in the all-Negro revue *Africana*, in 1927, and she followed this with other revues—*Lew Leslie's Blackbirds* in 1930 and *Rhapsody in Black* in 1931.

On with the Show was her first movie, which she made for Warners in 1929.

At the Cotton Club in 1933, Irving Berlin heard her sing

"Stormy Weather" and signed her for his successful musical *As Thousands Cheer*. The first Negro performer in an all-white cast on Broadway, she sang three of his songs, "Heat Wave," "Harlem on my Mind" and "Suppertime"—a song about a Southern woman whose husband had been lynched. In that song, Ethel portrayed the grief and anguish she had shared with a Negro family years before in Macon, Georgia, when their son was lynched.

In 1935 she performed with Beatrice Lillie in the revue *At Home Abroad*.

When Ethel started being billed as a "name performer," she had a little trick she would use when she didn't want to do a performance. She would ask for what she thought was an exorbitant salary. In the end, however, it only served to boost her salary and make her a very highly paid performer in later years.

Despite the recognition and acclaim she received, Ethel wasn't fulfilled. Her life, successful though it was, was a repetition of her youth, with no place to call home, living out of suitcases and keeping irregular schedules. What she wanted most was a sense of order, a nice quiet place to sleep, clean surroundings and good meals at regular times. Particularly in the early days, she used to dream about traveling around the world as a lady's maid to a kind and generous boss. In the meantime she continued to sing—her dream of an orderly, balanced life had to wait.

Her tumultuous emotional life didn't make for orderly living either. She was often in love, almost always with unsuitable or untrustworthy men—but only one man at a time. Ethel's hot temper often flared in these relationships.

Ethel didn't escape racial prejudice, even when she became a well-known star. She encountered it everywhere she went: in hotels, on Jim Crow railway trains and in night-clubs. Yet faced with blind bias and hatred, she never turned bitter or angry—she only felt pity for races that had to live in terror of each other. "I've never been sorry I'm colored. Suffering isn't prejudice. Just because a person is white doesn't mean he doesn't have trouble too," she once said.

Even as a well-known singer and entertainer, she wasn't elated about performing for a white audience. She was afraid they wouldn't grasp her distinctive delivery of the blues. When her own people liked her, it was obvious. "They'd scream, stomp, and applaud until the whole building shook," Ethel remembered. By contrast, the white folks were quiet and subdued with their clapping. Later, after years of singing to white audiences, Ethel changed her mind. Negro audiences upset her with their noisy response and their ribald shouts and cheers.

At the top of her career Ethel was performing at such elite nightclubs as the Embassy Club in New York City. Her clear, vibrant voice was singing such songs as "Go Back Where You Stayed Last Night," "You Can't Do What My Last Man Did," and "Heebie Jeebies." "No one could do the shimmies like I did, but I was never vulgar," she recalled. "In fact, although the shimmy was banned in Atlantic City, they let me do mine."

Ethel was always generous to her family and to people she loved. At one point she offered to take in the eighteen-month-old baby of a friend who could no longer care for the child. With no legal obligation involved, Ethel and the girl's mother agreed to allow Algretta to choose whom she wanted to live with when the child was old enough to make up her own mind. Ethel cared for Algretta until she was twelve, and later she supported in some way about twenty girls.

Ethel found the role of mother very satisfying and fulfilling. Years later she said in her autobiography, *His Eye Is on the Sparrow*, "My ambition was to bring Algretta up so everyone would love her as I'd never been loved as a little girl. . . . Being a mother is what makes a real life for a woman, not applause, your picture in the paper, the roses and the telegrams you get on opening night. A great many people who think of themselves as poor have the richness in their lives. You are a person of the greatest importance when you are a mother of a family. Just do your job right and your kids will love you. And for that love of theirs there is no satisfying substitute."

In 1939 Ethel became the first Negro woman to star in a dramatic play on Broadway. At the Empire Theatre, where so many great actresses had played, Ethel played the part of Hagar in *Mamba's Daughters*. The character of Hagar was so similar to her mother, Louise, that she could easily identify with her. The response on opening night was thunderous—seventeen curtain calls.

Back in the dressing room, Ethel recalled in *His Eye Is on the Sparrow*, "I burst into sobbing as I humbly thanked my God. Because even if no one else knew it, I had been no actress that night. I had only been remembering and all I had done was carry out His orders. And I had shown them all what it is to be a colored woman, dumb, ignorant, all boxed up and feeling everything with such intenseness that she is half crazy."

The critics praised her to the skies—all except Brooks Atkinson of the *New York Times*. In response her friends—who included Judith Anderson, Tallulah Bankhead, Cass Canfield, Dorothy Gish, Edwin Knopf—got together and took out an ad in the *Times* praising her performance:

"We, the undersigned, feel that Ethel Waters' superb performance in *Mamba's Daughters* . . . is a profound emotional experience which any playgoer would be the poorer for missing. It seems indeed to be such a magnificent example of great acting, simple, deeply felt, moving on a plane of complete reality, that we are glad to pay for the privilege of saying so."

The result was that Brooks Atkinson saw the play again and changed his mind!

Ethel Waters at age 7. On one of my Saturday visits, she reached for this picture asking with a gleam in her eye, "Guess who this is." Someone had found the picture and sent it to her. She immediately wanted copies made and sent to her friends across the country.

Above: an early picture of Ethel as Sweet Mama Stringbean.

Ethel's 21st birthday portrait—in color. "Would you like a copy?" she asked me when she showed me. "A would Bill and Joan [Brown] like one too?"

Anton Bruel's photo
from *Vanity Fair* of
Ethel singing "Heat Wave"
in Irving Berlin's
As Thousands Cheer.

Right: Carl Van Vechten's
1933 "Stormy Weather"
portrait.

WASHTUBS MEAN BLUE MONDAYS, BUT NOT WHEN ETHEL WATERS SINGS ABOUT
THEM.

Above is an artist's recollection of Ethel Waters, the stage's leading Negro feminine star, as she sings "Washtub Rub-sody," a feature of Lew Leslie's "Rhapsody in Black," which opens at the Shubert theater tonight.

Left: Cartoon by Vernon
Hampton with the heading
"Washtubs Mean Blue Mon-
days But Not When Ethel
Sings About Them." The cap-
tion reads: "Above is an artist's recollection of Ethel
Waters, the stage's leading
Negro feminine star, as she
sings 'Washtub Rub-sody,' a
feature of Lew Leslie's 'Rhapsody in Black,' which opens at
the Shubert theater tonight."

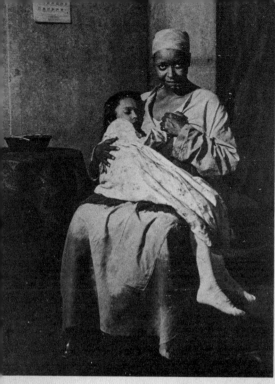

In 1939 Ethel starred as
Hagar in the play
Mamba's Daughters, a
role that brought her
the highest acclaim as
an actress.

Ethel gave this 1939 oil
painting by Luini
Lucioni to the
Grady Wilsons.

Above left: Portrait by Murray Kempton. Right: This 1940 charcoal portrait now hangs in Bill Brown's office. Below: In the movie version of *Cabin in the Sky*, Ethel played with Eddie "Rochester" Anderson, Lena Horne, and Louis Armstrong.

Top: A scene from the movie version of *The Member of the Wedding*, showing Ethel with Julie Harris.
Above: Ethel starred in the movie *Pinky* with Jeanne Crain, a role which won her an Academy Award nomination for best supporting actress. (*Brown Brothers photo*.)
Right: In her later years, Ethel appeared in an episode or two of a number of TV series, including *Daniel Boone*, *Owen Marshall* and others.

"Being Hagar softened me," Ethel continued. "I was able to make more allowance for the shortcomings of others. Before that I'd always been cursing outside and crying inside. Playing in *Mamba's Daughters* enabled me to rid myself of the terrible inward pressure, the flood of tears I'd been storing up ever since childhood."

Another time she commented about her acting ability: "I'm an actress who doesn't just learn a role. I just turn a page of memory and portray something from life. I act instinctively. That's why I can't play any role that isn't based on something in my life."

After Ethel and the company took *Mamba's Daughters* on tour, the role of Petunia, the loving and faithful wife in *Cabin in the Sky*, came her way in 1940. It was in this musical she sang the song by Vernon Blake, "Taking a Chance on Love," as well as the title song. Critics called it the best performance of her career, and said so again when she played the part for director Vincente Minnelli in the film version.

Ethel loved the feeling of owning—of having a place to call her own, and while she was in Hollywood in 1942, she bought a house in Los Angeles. She always lived simply, but she enjoyed the comforts of fur coats, jewelry, and big cars, insisting that her fans expected it of her.

Before *Cabin* had been released, she had made her *Tales of Manhattan* and followed that with *Cairo*, using what little time was left for wartime radio performances with the USO. However, during the 1940s Ethel's movie career began to slide. She still had engagements at nightclubs, but no one offered her parts in plays or movies, and any that came her way fell through. She began to get depressed. But in 1949 she played the role of grandmother in 20th Century Fox's *Pinky*, for which she received an Oscar nomination.

Her next big break came in 1950 when she got the dramatic part of the cook in *The Member of the Wedding*, which also starred Julie Harris and Brandon DeWilde. For this again she received much acclaim and the New York Drama Critics Award. She was nominated for an Academy Award for the best supporting role of the film version in 1955.

In the play and the movie she sang "His Eye Is on the Sparrow," and the song became her trademark. However, as the play was originally written, the cook, Berenice Sadie Brown, was a hard, bitter woman and was to sing a Russian lullaby. But Ethel refused the part unless there was God in the play, and she was free to put her own interpretation on the part, which included changing the song.

Recalling the pre-play discussions in *To Me It's Wonderful,* Ethel commented, "I had never heard tell of a colored woman, especially from Georgia, who had ever sung a Russian ditty to a child!"

What song would she sing? Carson McCullers, the playwright, asked her.

Ethel warned her it had the name of Jesus in it, which some people didn't like, but she'd be willing to omit the verse and sing only the chorus.

" 'Will you sing it all—now, please?'

"I started to sing, right there where I was sitting, and went all the way through 'His Eye Is on the Sparrow.'

"When I finished, including the verse with the name of Jesus in it, there was a long silence in that room, except that Carson McCullers had crossed the room and was in my lap, crying."

After her success with *Member,* Ethel was offered the opportunity of getting in on the ground floor of a new medium —television. She was given the starring role in the weekly series, "Beulah." But the series died and film parts became scarce again. Her career seemed finished as ill-advised investments, tax problems, and untrustworthy agents led to her suddenly being out of demand as an entertainer.

"Where I come from," she explained, "people don't get

close enough to money to keep a working acquaintance with it . . . so I didn't know how to keep it."

She made *The Heart Is a Rebel* for World Wide Pictures, and her last film, *The Sound and the Fury*, was made in 1958. She appeared occasionally in television roles for such programs as "Route 66" and "Daniel Boone."

At the lowest point in her career, when she felt she had had it all and lost it all, Ethel went to see her mother. For the first time Momweeze really encouraged her. Ethel recounted their conversation in *His Eye Is on the Sparrow.*

"My mother looked at me with love in her eyes and said, 'Ethel, I'm glad you've come. I want you to know that, even if you never see me again. You've been a good girl. You know God and He has His arms around you. . . .

" 'You really took a beating. But don't you worry none, because you're coming back. . . . '

"That was the acceptance and the fulfillment I'd been dreaming of winning all my life. . . . For the first time I knew then that Momweeze loved me."

Momweeze was right. Ethel was to come back better than ever!

"God don't sponsor no flops."

Chapter Three

"GOD DON'T SPONSOR NO FLOPS."

That was Ethel Waters's response when her friends Tex McCrary and Jinx Falkenberg asked her on their New York radio program if the forthcoming Billy Graham Crusade was going to be a success.

Not only did she firmly believe it was going to be successful, but she went on to predict that Madison Square Garden was going to be full and the meetings would be extended.

Ethel had never met Billy Graham or attended one of his meetings. But she had listened to him on the radio. When she finally saw a picture of him, she first thought he was "too young and too good looking to be trusted. And I was slightly annoyed that he was white." In her mind she questioned whether white people could have the same zeal for Jesus and the Bible as her folk did.

But the lanky North Carolina evangelist was getting through to her. "He didn't use a whole gang of Amens and Hallelujahs. Yet he spoke in a language my intellect could comprehend." "And the Bible says . . ." was his favorite phrase, so maybe he wasn't a phony.

Although Ethel still had her home in Los Angeles, she had been living in New York for some time. At this time she was hoping to do another stint of *Member of the Wedding* with a stock cast. She also had a couple of her one-woman shows— *An Evening with Ethel Waters*—to do but demands for her performances were not many.

When Lane Adams, a member of the Billy Graham Team, heard Ethel's remarks on the radio show, he phoned to offer her tickets to the crusade. She readily accepted them— aisle ones in the loge where the seats were comfortable and wide enough to accommodate her 350 pounds.

Ethel Waters entered Madison Square Garden that night in 1957 a disillusioned, lonely, sixty-one-year-old woman. She had become successful at giving out happiness, but her personal life lacked peace. She was in debt, was having physical problems, as well as being much too heavy to perform comfortably, and was worried about her career.

When she entered the Garden, she was amazed at the transformation. She had played there often for benefit shows when the noisy, unruly crowds jammed the gates until opening and then shoved in to find seats. But this crowd exhibited a peace and serenity while waiting and listening to the choir rehearse "Blessed Assurance," a song she had learned in her little church in Chester.

That night she hung onto every word Billy Graham said. "What he said seemed like he was answering every question I had in my mind," she recalled. "Above all he kept saying how close the Lord is to you. I began thinking along a different trend, that God wasn't far away—it was me shutting him out." The more he talked the more she knew the Lord was calling her to "come back home."

All her life she had felt caught and confused between her mother's staunch Protestantism and her grandmother's Catholicism. She knew that she loved God and He loved her, but she never had the feeling of peace with Jesus. As she went back to her hotel room that night she felt as though a weight had been lifted from her heart.

Night after night she attended the crusade meetings, but finally the strain of waiting in line before each service was too much for her. The second week of the crusade she called Lane Adams to ask if there wasn't an easier way to get in. She had seen people wearing buttons and badges walk right through the lines.

Lane suggested she join the choir and then with her red button there would be no waiting in line. She smugly got her button with no intention of singing with the choir. But she was trapped. A secretary was waiting to escort her to the alto section.

Bill Brown, associate crusade director at that crusade, recalls with laughter the dilemma that faced him when told that Ethel Waters, with well over 350 pounds, would be singing in the choir:

We felt honored to have her but we wished there was a little less of her—the seats in the choir section were designed for people of normal proportions. I first thought of taking the arm off the end of the row, but I knew only half of her would fit on the seat and with such a hangover she would be uncomfortable. Besides we were warned by the fire marshal not to block the aisles. I felt proud of myself when I came up with the idea of taking the second arm out, thereby making it possible for Ethel to occupy two seats at one time. Would you believe, even with that she still had to do some squeezing! The RESERVED sign kept that double seat waiting for that very special choir member each night.

Ethel said of her experience of singing in the choir, "Cliff Barrows proceeded to have me being like a jumping jack. I'd hardly get down in the seat before he'd have me up standing with the choir. I always felt that Cliff with his eagle eye was watching my mouth which was loud, wrong and strong. I didn't know how to read music, so when they rehearsed a hymn that I didn't know, I'd just work my mouth."

Cliff Barrows clearly remembers that time in New York in 1957, as he recalls Ethel Waters joining his massive choir:

She had been with us almost every night for six weeks, and I purposely did not refer to her being in the choir, since it was obvious to us she wanted to participate without being singled out and made reference to. I appreciated her spirit in this regard and certainly respected her wishes. When the time came for us to extend the meetings, I asked her quickly in front of the choir one evening if she would be willing to sing for us. Immediately the choir broke out in spontaneous applause affirming their desire as well, and of course, she graciously consented to do so.

I think one of the moving experiences of my life was leading her that first time in singing with the choir, "His Eye Is on the Sparrow." She did it so beautifully and seemed so obviously moved in her own heart and spirit, and I felt that the entire choir along with all of us on the music staff were caught up in it. Of course, during the next two-and-a-half months we sang it many times, and also worked on a couple of other songs which she and the choir sang. We had her appear at least once a week for the rest of the crusade, which went for four months.

Ethel recalled on the Word record *Just a Little Talk with Ethel* that she was scared to say yes to Cliff Barrows's request, because a woman had never sung at a crusade, but also because she couldn't really call herself a Christian—and besides she didn't have what she called "a church voice." Yet she wanted to stand up and publicly claim the Lord. If she sang "Sparrow," she would be making a public commitment, and she couldn't go back to show business.

"I was afraid of losing the feeling I had now. If I went back I wouldn't have the incentive to get up on stage and sing some of the songs I knew I could put across that the public still loved hearing.

"Oh, when I was in show business, I was religious. I thanked Jesus each time for helping me please the people. But I hadn't faced that you're to completely relinquish yourself—you can't serve two masters, and the stage don't fit in. But it was my livelihood. And how could I make my living without it?

"But the long and the short of it was, I did sing 'Sparrow.' And the Lord has made me rich since then! I'm not talking financially. But I have found in Him everything I need. I feel secure. I never had that shoulder and lap, but I have it now in my spiritual strength and faith in Him. I have many laps— my children I wouldn't have known if I hadn't met Jesus."

When the crusade was over, Ethel returned to her home in Los Angeles. She was concerned as to how she could pay her mounting debts, but she trusted God to supply all her needs. She sold her home to make room for the freeway, and this provided her with the money to pay all her bills. She then shared a home with Donna and Elwood Wilson, who personally looked after her for over six years.

"Theatre and professional life is borrowed time. I don't care who you are," she said. "After you get to the top of the mountain, you can't stay there. You got to descend, and that doesn't mean you're no good. But there's no place for you up there. The only thing that is eternal and everlasting is Jesus Christ."

Cy Jackson, who had first seen Ethel in Des Moines, Iowa, in 1955, when she appeared at the Radio Theatre in *Member of the Wedding*, tells of his association with her:

It was shortly after the Billy Graham Crusade in Madison Square Garden that I contacted Ethel about being the headliner at a concert I was involved in with Ralph Carmichael at Red Rocks amphitheatre near Denver. She was at that time living in New York City. She was quite hesitant about accepting the invitation, and I recall giving her every argument in the book, and then it took another phone call or two to get an affirmative answer. The big question in her mind seemed to be how she could justify singing in a sacred concert (which was to be her first) and still not leave the impression she was just cashing in on the publicity she had received at the Garden crusade. But the vibes must have been right—she accepted on the basis of doing "Sparrow" and perhaps one other sacred number. She appeared in the concert and I know that her name very definitely was instrumental in giving us a capacity crowd of over ten thousand people.

In August of 1957 she arrived in Denver for the concert. I'll never forget as we met her at the airplane—all 350 pounds of her—the first thing she said to me was, "Well, here is your big fat sparrow"! I recall the evening following a rehearsal that we returned to the hotel and she took a seat on one of the chairs at the entrance of the hotel. Her weight was just too much for that chair—she and the chair both went down! It took several of us to get her up.

One of the first concerts Ethel did for her Lord was in Fresno, California. Dan Jantz, president and manager of the Fresno Bible House, sponsored the evening with Ethel. He remembers the night:

We rented the Roosevelt High School Auditorium which seats approximately twenty-six hundred people, and we began to advertise the concert and that Ethel Waters would be appearing in person in Fresno.

It was on a no-admission-charge basis, so we had no idea how many people would come. Before the concert began, the auditorium was filled to capacity. It was exciting to see the eager looks on the faces of the people just waiting to get a glimpse of Ethel Waters. Most of them had never seen her before, but knew her through her radio, television and theatrical appearances, and they were most anxious to see and hear her in person.

I remember meeting Ethel backstage and telling her, "Ethel, the place is packed and everyone is waiting to hear you."

She replied, "Well, glory be, they are going to get an earful tonight, because I feel like singing hallelujah tonight. My heart is overflowing."

Just the way she said it, I thought she would start singing backstage. I felt I had very little time for any kind of introduction, because I thought she'd come bouncing on the stage at any time. Just about that time, the curtain went up and all I did was come on stage to say, "Ladies and gentlemen, Ethel Waters." Everybody rose to their feet as she walked on stage singing the chorus of "His Eye Is on the Sparrow."

During intermission when she came backstage, she told me, "I'm having a ball." She also told me she did not know how she could get along without Cy and Vera Jackson who were her escorts on this engagement as well as many others since that time.

Needless to say, Ethel Waters won the hearts of her listeners in Fresno. She had the audience laughing, crying, joining in and singing with her . . . what a night!

Shortly thereafter, Ethel recorded her first of three albums for Word, Inc. Cy Jackson recalls that she had a pretty good business head. "What's on the rail for the lizard?" she asked when it came time to talk about contracts.

For that first record, Ethel chose her favorite songs and spirituals, many of which had never been put down on paper before. She sang them to the arranger, Paul Mickelson, and he wrote the score. Among them was the Negro spiritual "I Just Can't Stay Here by Myself," which tells the story of a slave mother whose children were sold as slaves and who pleaded to be sold along with her last child. When Ethel was recording that spiritual and the song "Mammy," she broke down and wept, as the songs called up the pains and sorrows of her childhood and as she felt her own mother's and grandmother's experiences.

Another song on the record was "Partners with God," which she wrote herself with a young composer, Eddie Stuart, who heard her say one time, "I could never be destitute as long as I am partners with God."

During these years Ethel did concerts in churches, Youth for Christ meetings, conventions, etc. She was accompanied in many of these engagements by Dick Bolks and Paul DeKorte. The two men would sing and play during the early part of the program, and then Dick would accompany Ethel during her part.

In the spring of 1964, Ethel did a revival of *The Member of the Wedding* at the Pasadena Playhouse, Pasadena, California. Scheduled to run two weeks, the engagement ran five weeks and set house box office records. As a result, she followed with *Member* at the LaJolla Playhouse and the Lobero Theatre in Santa Barbara. Later she did a run of the play in a dinner theatre in Chicago. These were all successful engagements, but because of her health, she could not continue the heavy grind, even though booking agents continued to stay on her heels to get commitments for continuing to play in *Member*.

Cy Jackson continues his memories of Ethel:

In November in the early sixties, Ethel presented her one-woman show, An Evening with Ethel Waters, at the Sombrero Playhouse in Phoenix. She was interviewed by the Phoenix Gazette, and they asked her what she planned to do Thanksgiving Day. "Stay in my hotel room alone," she answered. A Christian family read the story and invited her to dine with them on Thanksgiving. She was elated and im-

pressed that someone—strangers—just for the sake of Christian love would ask her to their home. She graciously and humbly accepted their invitation.

My wife Vera and I would often take her to eat at her favorite cafeteria in Pasadena—Beadle's. She liked it because the menu included her favorite—halibut. The love for halibut stayed with her, and when she was unable to leave her apartment, I would take her the halibut every couple of weeks, along with another favorite of hers—pumpkin pie. It would give us a chance to sit and talk—and me to take in those verbal gems for which she will be long remembered.

Grady Wilson, an associate evangelist with Billy Graham, and his wife Wilma were two of Ethel's closest friends. "Grady understands me," Ethel often told me on returning from singing at his crusades. She loved his sense of humor, and the two of them shared many belly laughs. However, one of Grady's fondest memories of Ethel is a serious one, about the time she helped bridge the racial gap in Barbados.

At a press conference prior to a crusade in Barbados, a reporter asked Ethel, "Miss Waters, don't you feel ill-treated in the United States because of your color?" In her frank and honest way she replied "Oh no, baby, no. It's about time instead of hating we start loving whitey." The next day the local newspaper headlined her response: "Ethel Waters pleads with Barbadians to stop hating and start loving." It pleased Ethel that "they got the message."

Ethel loved doing sacred concerts across the nation. They were squeezed in between the Billy Graham Crusades which were her first love.

When Billy Graham was going to hold a crusade in the Cow Palace in San Francisco, Ethel called Cliff Barrows and asked if she could come. He was glad to have her and let her sing each night.

From then on she watched *Decision* magazine for the crusade schedule. "I didn't wait for you to call me," she told Cliff Barrows, "I called you." A taping of the "Route 66" TV show delayed her going to Philadelphia, but when her schedule was free to go she called Cliff and shouted, "I'm coming on my own steam."

Ethel Waters became a familiar sight at Billy Graham Crusades as she sang in Boston, Chicago, Honolulu, Charlotte and Greenville.

The Rev. T. Eugene Coffin, executive pastor of Garden Grove Community Church recalls the time when, as minister of Whittier Friends Church, he was invited to participate in worship service at the White House to which Ethel was also invited.

Just before the limousine came to take them to the executive mansion, Mr. Coffin and his wife invited Ethel into their hotel room for a prayer that God might use them in this great opportunity to touch so many lives. As they bowed their heads, Ethel said to Mr. Coffin, "You pray. I'm all prayed up."

Prayer to Ethel was a most important element of her life. Her prayer life, she often said, was "a continual running conversation with my precious Jesus."

Ethel Waters never really left show business—she just changed her message. She told everyone who would listen about her precious Savior. "He loves each and every one of you—and so do I," she told audiences. "As long as He lets me, I'm going to spend the rest of my days openly praising Him."

"I know rabbits and rabbits' habits," Ethel used to say. She had people all figured out.

Chapter Four

UNTIL 1966 THE ONLY KNOWLEDGE I had of Ethel Waters was from hearing and seeing her on a Billy Graham telecast. My little world in Correctionville, Iowa, did not include the arts, or music of artists of Waters's calibre. Her movies and plays had never reached my hometown.

When I graduated from high school, my dreams were big as I left family and friends to make it on my own in the metropolis of Minneapolis. After graduation from business college, I obtained a job at the Billy Graham headquarters. There I was a bashful secretary among hundreds of other employees, easily impressed by any dignitaries that visited the office.

It seemed amazing to me, and one of God's mysterious ways of working, that I, who had never traveled beyond our neighboring states, was selected to work in crusades all across the country from California to New York. It was exciting to see our great United States. It was even more exciting when I was singled out to transfer to Atlanta, Georgia, to work in the Team office there.

It was while I was working at Billy Graham's crusade in

Greenville, South Carolina, that I got the chance to meet Ethel Waters in person. The theatrical accomplishments of this talented woman were so far removed from my experience that I could hardly appreciate them. I was, however, awed to meet this singer who was thrilling the crusade audiences night after night. The kindness and loving concern she showed to this shy country gal, even in our first brief meeting, left me with a warm feeling.

At the conclusion of the ten-day crusade, I was assigned to take Ethel to the airport. I was excited but also worried—how would this lady of 280 pounds fit into my little green Corvair? I also wondered how a woman of her stature would feel being seen riding in my old jalopy, because I assumed she was used to riding in limousines and fancy chauffeured cars. After all, she lived in the Hollywood area, and wasn't that how famous people lived?

Climbing into the front seat and without an inch to spare, she settled into my car. (The front seat was as far back as it would go and I had to stretch to reach the pedals.) She chuckled and didn't seem to mind a bit that we weren't riding in style. In fact, quite the contrary, she seemed grateful for the transportation. Somehow I sensed she knew that my taking her to the airport was the thrill of my lifetime, and the pleasure this gave her was worth the discomfort.

At the airport, I timidly asked if I might take her picture.

"Sure," she replied and graciously posed for me and my instamatic in front of the Greenville/Spartanburg Airport. The hug she gave me as she left was tender and caring, making me feel like a princess.

From that first encounter I was adopted into her "family." Although Mom had been married several times, she never had children of her own. If she took a liking to you, you automatically were one of her "babies." The list ranged from former President Richard Nixon, Julie Harris, Ruth and Billy Graham, Sammy Davis, Jr., Carol Channing, Grady Wilson and Cliff Barrows, on to her faithful mailman Ernie Chavez, to housewives, secretaries, servicemen, etc. However, for some reason there were those who never became part of the family. If Ethel thought someone was using her for their own good or "cashing in on her name," she could take an instant dislike to that person. She detested "freeloaders" and could spot a phony a mile away. "I know rabbits and rabbits' habits," she used to say. She had people all figured out.

I continued to cross paths with Ethel at various crusades from London to Los Angeles.

In the fall of 1969 I left my work with the Billy Graham Crusades to devote full time to interior design school in Los Angeles. That Christmas I called Ethel to wish her a "Merry Christmas." She asked if I would have any spare time to help with a few projects. "Sure," I said, "but not until after the holidays and school finals."

When things settled down in the new year, I finally got around to calling her, only to get a recording, "This number is no longer in service and there is no new number." I thought I had come to a dead end since I knew she had an unlisted number.

When I was asked to return to temporary work at the Billy Graham Crusade in New York City in the summer of 1970, Ethel was there to sing at the Shea stadium meetings, so we were united once again.

She seemed delighted to see me and gave me her new unlisted phone number. She had moved from her large home in Los Angeles into an apartment at the Bunker Hill Towers. When we returned to Los Angeles, I kept my promise and called to make a date when I could come to help her with her work. I had no idea what lay ahead.

On a hot July afternoon, I parked my car at the downtown skyscraper and timidly told the doorman, "Ethel Waters is expecting me."

He graciously opened the door, and I sank to my ankles in

the plush rust carpeting in the lobby. Surveying the surroundings as I waited for the elevator, I noticed the elaborate chandelier, the brightly colored oil paintings and a wall of mirrors.

A tingle of excitement welled up in me as I rode up to the fifteenth floor. I rang the bell at #1502 and was promptly greeted by a familiar friendly "hi." I was immediately at ease with this woman whose love just seemed to radiate everywhere.

She ushered me into her living room with its green shag carpeting. Since I was studying interior design, I was intrigued by the aqua Queen Anne chair, the Victorian sofa flanked by identical gold chairs with carved wood, and the antique carved coffee table with the glass top. The walls were lined with awards she had received through the years. I was amused at the scores of pictures and paintings of herself on every wall and available shelf space. Even the centers of her telephone dials were covered by pictures of her. "That's so no one visiting me can ask to use my phone and find out my number."

For years to come, whenever I was at a loss as to what to give her as a birthday or Christmas gift, any picture of her blown up to 8x10 and framed was a sure winner.

A baby grand piano, littered with mail, was in the corner of the tiny apartment. Ethel admitted she couldn't play it and couldn't even read a note of music. In fact, she picked up a piece of sheet music and asked if I could tell her what key it was in. (My flute lessons in high school paid off at that moment.)

Ethel took a seat in her black leather swivel chair next to the window. (Later I was to realize Ethel spent most of her waking hours in this chair, listening to her portable TV and the radio, often both at the same time!) I sat opposite her and was enthralled at the view. Her apartment overlooked the beautiful Los Angeles Music Center and the busy web of highways that make up the interchange of the Pasadena, Hollywood and San Bernardino Freeways, with the mountains in the background. The hustle and the bustle of the busy world beneath her was a sharp contrast to the peace and tranquility in her little three-room "nest," as she called it.

As we chatted away, Ethel pulled out from a nearby shelf boxes containing thousands of Christmas, Easter, Valentine, Mother's Day and birthday cards from her fans and friends. She had saved these over many years, and they were just too meaningful and beautiful for her to part with them. She asked if I could find a use for them. She knew that pasted into scrapbooks together with the fact that they had belonged to her, they would bring joy to patients in hospitals and old folks homes. She loved receiving fan mail, and in later years, when it became necessary for me to read her mail to her because her eyesight was so bad, she would be deeply moved by the homage people paid to her. Often I would see tears in her eyes as she heard the accolades given to her. Sometimes she would ask me to read the letters twice. "Isn't that just beautiful?" she would say. "They don't have to take the time to write me such nice things."

Knowing that she hated the word *black* when referring to her race, I would often change *black* to *Negro* when I read the letters. Once she stopped me short. "Twila, did that say *black* or *Negro*?" she asked. I had to admit I had changed it, which only led me to the conclusion that someway she was reading those letters before I read them to her.

She would stack the mail on the little table by the window, and on Saturday morning visits I would sort through it. Some of her mail would be forwarded from her agent, Sid Levee, and some would be sent from the Billy Graham Association in Minneapolis.

One man tried a unique approach. He sent a letter to her in care of Mr. Richard M. Nixon, President of the United States, 1600 Pennsylvania Ave., Washington. D.C. It worked!

She got it! This really amused Ethel. She thought the man was clever to use such an idea, but refused to make it known as she didn't want others to try it and make a nuisance of themselves and trouble her "precious child, the President."

Besides the usual requests for autographs, which she generally ignored unless she received a stamped envelope, Ethel got requests for pictures and personal possessions for charity auctions. She was deeply touched by a beautiful letter from a Mrs. Parker asking for a thimble for a collection. Ethel, in a rare mood, pointed to her sewing box and asked me to look for one. I found two and she chose one to send.

The thank-you from Mrs. Parker said, "You really are a dear! Today when I opened the letter which included the thimble, I cried. I could not hold back the tears. I always cry when I'm overjoyed and happy. I was so elated. Words are inadequate to express my thanks and appreciation to you. I shall cherish the thimble but will always cherish your beautiful life."

As the in-between person, I was thrilled to see Ethel happy for Mrs. Parker's words of praise, and a seemingly insignificant object leaving a beautiful impression on a fan.

Ethel also got beautiful letters from young people. A twelve-year-old boy, Scott, was infatuated by her. He had bought all her books and albums, and corresponded regularly with her. I was amused as he added a P.S. on the outside of one envelope.

"Miss Waters, you know what? Well, I went to the fish market and I got a black goldfish, named it Sweet Mama Stringbean."

This was the world of Ethel Waters. On one hand, she had a vast family of fans and well-wishers throughout the world. On the other hand, here was a woman often staying for days in her small apartment, living one of the loneliest and set-apart lives I'd ever seen.

As my first visit to Ethel's apartment progressed, she

asked if I could sew. I answered in the affirmative, thinking she just wanted me to sew a torn seam or hem a dress for her. When she walked over to the coffee table and picked up three pieces of fabric, I gulped, trying to think of something nice to say about the gaudy orange and beige floral prints. To my amazement, Ethel asked if I would make her a dress from one of the pieces of material. I hemmed and hawed around, not having too much confidence in my sewing, since I had only sewn clothes for myself. Here was a lady who at one time had spent small fortunes on gowns and had famous designer dresses, and she was asking me to make a dress for her?

"Oh, Twila, you can do it," she urged. "You won't have any problem making a simple shift dress, sleeveless and with pockets."

"Well," I hesitated, "I guess I can try. I'll have to have the pattern for it."

"You can make it exactly like this one," Ethel said as she slipped off the dress she was wearing and handed it to me.

Even though this wise woman did not have much formal schooling, she knew psychology! She convinced me I *could* do it if I tried. I wasn't about to let her down.

I left her apartment that afternoon with the fabric in one hand and her book, *His Eye Is on the Sparrow*, in the other. It wasn't until I finished reading that book that I began to understand a little about the complex Ethel Waters.

Up to that point I had no idea of the struggle and suffering she had endured growing up in the slums. It was beyond my comprehension what it was like to be a Negro and have to fight to be accepted, let alone be respected and admired by white people. I had never known vast fortunes and what it was like to lose one. I came to understand why Ethel could not trust everybody and how she longed to be loved for herself.

Back in my apartment, I measured and figured and came

up with a paper tissue pattern. My nerves were on edge as I took that first scissor snip into the material. I didn't have a clue as to how I could ever replace the fabric if things went wrong. Consequently, I made sure there was plenty of seam allowance. My roommate nicknamed me "Omar, the tent-maker" as I cut and sewed the largest dress I had ever made.

The next week I took the dress back to Ethel's for a fitting, and held my breath as she tried it on. So far so good. It was what she wanted, and with a dart here and a tuck there it would fit.

This taught me a great lesson—one of the many I was to learn from this wise teacher. My sewing was not that great and I knew without a doubt many people could have done a much better job. However, because I was willing to do my best, the job was accomplished.

I made several other dresses for Ethel, but the real challenge came when she couldn't part with the beautiful paisley print of the lining of a worn-out raincoat. "It will make a real sharp outfit," she convinced me. You can imagine my delight when I saw her interviewed by Merv Griffin on TV wearing that creation.

Oh, yes, I learned also to make the matching hats. These were a trademark with Ethel, but the real reason she never appeared in public without one of her scarves was that she was going bald on top and she wanted to hide the fact.

As the months wore on, Ethel became more and more like a real mother to me. "Mom" was what she was in fact rather than just a name I called her. Regardless of the difference in color, I was the daughter she never had. I had grown to love her deeply. Almost every Saturday morning I would trek downtown and be greeted cheerfully by the doorman who had come to expect my weekly visit with her.

Occasionally I would take Ethel shopping. I loved the attention we received when we were out together. I particularly remember one time we were looking for bedspreads in a

Sears store. We had gone our separate ways in the bedding department when I heard Ethel say, "Twi, come here and see what you think about this one." When I joined her, the sales clerks gave each other quizzical, confused looks. They knew Ethel Waters, but who was this young white girl she treated like a daughter? It was only at times like this, when I realized that other people had a problem, that I was aware of the difference in the color of our skins.

Ethel's great love was giving. She found her joy living by the Scripture verse, "It is better to give than receive." Hardly a time went by that I walked out of her apartment without something in my arms. If it wasn't money (gas money as she called it), it was one of her prized possessions. I learned to accept her gifts graciously, knowing how much it meant to her that I was thrilled at getting them. "Could you use this?" she would say as she handed me a box of used wrapping paper and torn ribbons. I received outdated purses, huge vases and baskets for floral arrangements, and odds and ends of dishes. Once she gave me five bowls that to me just looked like old-fashioned dishes. I used them for my breakfast cereal every day for several years before I learned the value of those Limoges bowls.

When Ethel learned that she could trust me completely and rely on me, she wanted to reward me. She took me to her bedroom and said, "I've been thinking about this for a couple of days and have decided I want you to have this." Then opening her closet door she pulled out a flowing beige and yellow negligee someone had given to her. It was beautiful, all chiffon, but at least size Extra Large. She made me promise I wouldn't wear it as a nightgown but would make it into an evening dress for myself. Every now and then I get it out and look it over, but I haven't yet figured a way to make it into a formal dress size 9.

Mom's great love of giving rather than receiving made it extremely difficult on special occasions to come up with a gift idea for her. On one birthday, my roommate, Nancy

Moyer, and I prepared a gift certificate "Good for one thorough house-cleaning at a mutually convenient time." We couldn't have given her anything that would have pleased her more. Since her health was failing, it was difficult for her to do her regular household chores, and it worried her that the dusting and vacuuming were not getting done. For years after that I heard her tell others, "Those two precious children gave their time to come down and clean my place."

Here was another lesson I learned from the ever-wise Waters. One of the greatest gifts you can give a person, especially an elderly person, is your time.

One Saturday before Mother's Day I wracked my brain trying to figure out what little thing I could take Mom. After a special occasion such as this, I usually went home from her place with flower arrangements or perfume and powder. It was next to impossible to find something she would keep or use. I finally settled upon the idea of a pumpkin pie, one of her favorites, from Marie Callender's. It seemed like a silly gift but one in which I couldn't go wrong. She squealed with delight at the sight and smell of that pie when I walked in the door. Just before leaving her apartment that day, she handed me $5 and said, "Here, take this."

"What's that for?" I asked.

"Well, pies cost money," she replied.

"But," I stammered, "it's your Mother's Day present."

Since I never could win an argument with her, I sheepishly took the money. As usual, I had ended up on the receiving end while she did the giving. I had bought a gift for $1.95 and not only did she pay for her gift but I left with a profit of $3.05.

One of my Saturday chores with her was to help her with a bath. She was afraid to step in a tub of hot water when she was alone because the warm water relaxed her, often causing her to lose strength, and she worried whether she would be able to get out of the tub by herself.

It took a lot of concentration on my part to get the water

just the right temperature. I didn't like being blamed for getting the water too hot, so on this one morning I tried especially hard to do everything right. Ethel stepped in. The water was perfect! She sat down and let out a yelp. I had been so busy checking the temperature of the water that I failed to see that the lavender bath mat with rows and rows of tiny suction cups was upside down. Kneeling beside the tub I began to laugh as I visualized Mom standing up with the mat attached to her bottom and me pulling it off one suction cup at a time. Ethel was laughing too.

Through gales of laughter she said to me, "Twi, if you ever do this to me again, I'm gonna make you strip and get in here."

By now the tears were streaming down my face as I sat on the floor laughing at the predicament I had gotten her into. "Well," she grunted, "I've heard of turning the other cheek, but when *both cheeks* get it . . . !"

"People can still hurt me. Jesus never will."

Chapter Five

BECAUSE OF HER SIZE, Ethel didn't get out much, and because she didn't trust a lot of people, she didn't have many visitors. So she looked forward to what became my weekly visits, and began to depend on them.

Although I dearly loved Ethel, there were times when I really begrudged spending every Saturday morning with her. While my friends were going to the beach or having brunches, I was trekking down to the Bunker Hill Towers. I longed for a Saturday to sleep late, but I gave up that luxury because I felt a deep sense of responsibility to this lady who counted on me.

When I'd get to Ethel's apartment and see how eagerly she greeted me, I would feel guilty for resenting spending time with her. "Twila," she painfully admitted to me once, "some days I sit here all day long and have no one to talk to unless you call."

And there was something relaxing and soothing about her "little nest." Often I would forget about my hectic schedule and the world racing by as I sat across from her in my little chair by the window.

Some days it was like history unfolding before me. She

would reminisce about her childhood and how she got started in show business. I heard about the Jim Crow cars on the railroad and how when she would reach St. Louis she would have to move to the back of the train. She could chuckle now about having to eat her lunch in her car since the restaurant refused to serve a colored person.

"I know what I'm talking about," she would say in discussing some news item. She always kept abreast of the local and national news and was quick to debate anyone she could on current affairs. She held very strong opinions about most subjects. I could never win an argument with her, so I learned to nod my agreement and disagree silently. But as time went by, I discovered she was generally right. With her uncanny sixth sense, she could read between the lines.

Judging from the fan mail Ethel received, there were a number of people who would have loved to fill my shoes. It was a privilege to be "her baby girl," although many times I didn't feel so privileged.

I dreaded grocery shopping for her. She would see new products mentioned on TV and decide she had to have them. It might be a new brand of toilet cleaner or maybe it was a frozen cake. Whatever it was, it had to be the exact size and same brand—absolutely no substitutes! Often I had to go to at least three markets to find the right item.

When I would goof and bring the wrong thing, she couldn't seem to understand. "You should remember which kind it was. You got it for me the last time," she would say, not remembering that "the last time" may have been six months ago. Then she started saving boxes and wrappers so I would be sure to get the right item.

If I would forget to bring something she'd asked me to get, I would get a scolding. "Twila," she'd say, "you're young. You should have remembered to do that." Her own memory had always been fantastic.

But along with the scoldings, I got undeserved praise. We were being driven to the airport to return to Los Angeles from a crusade when another passenger in the car asked exactly what I did for World Wide Pictures. "Oh, I just type letters, answer the phones and stuff," I casually answered. "Don't let her tell you that," Ethel blurted to the passenger. "When Bill Brown isn't around she runs that place. When they need someone to work in another city, they send for Twila. She's a big shot." I was speechless as I suddenly discovered my job was so important.

Ethel was always interested in what I was doing. "Well, kiddo, what are you up to today?" she would ask. "Any big dates tonight?"

If I happened to mention I was having a special friend for dinner that night, it was not unusual for her to reach into her pocketbook and pull out a five- or a ten-dollar bill. "Here, have this one on me," she would say.

We joked that I couldn't introduce her to my boyfriends because she was too much competition for me. "Yeah, I'm a sex symbol," she would say, laughing. If a beau did meet her, she would always insist upon some "sugar" before he left. They were always eager to give her a hug and kiss—she had that special charm.

Ethel and I shared a love for beautiful clothes. "That's a sharp outfit, kiddo," she would say when I arrived. "Is it new?" If she thought my dress was too short or my blue jeans too tight, she would tell me that too.

Ernie, Ethel's faithful mailman and friend, would often arrive with the mail during my Saturday visits. He, too, had his weekly chores—watering and caring for her dearly loved plants.

One Saturday I was telling Ethel about the minor car accident I had been in. I was upset because it wasn't my fault, but because the other driver didn't have insurance I would have to pay $100 deductible. She knew this would be a strain for me.

"Well, I'm going to pay that," Ethel insisted.

"Oh, no, you don't need to do that," I said, embarrassed. I didn't want her to think I was telling her about it because I was hinting for the money.

"Well, I'm going to," she declared. "That's what moms are for."

At that moment I realized how important it was for her to be my Mom. It made her feel needed and it was a tremendous financial boost for me, so we both were winners.

One Saturday I announced to Ethel that my roommate and I were each going to get our own apartment. Because of the rising price of gasoline we felt it wiser if we were each closer to our offices. Since I had never had an unfurnished apartment before, Ethel wanted to help furnish my little abode.

On my next visit, Ethel had boxes of appliances and kitchen items packed for me. I fell heir to an electric coffeepot, an electric fry pan, an egg poacher ("Twila, the way you like to cook and entertain, I can't imagine that you've never fixed poached eggs!"), a vacuum cleaner, bath towels (marked HIS and HERS), and a transparent 8 x 10 color photograph of Billy Graham equipped with a light and electrical cord. Unfortunately, I never found a place for that!

That was only the beginning. She wanted to know, since it was only a one-bedroom apartment, if I had found a hide-a-bed for my living room. She knew I had a lot of out-of-town friends and would need to provide them with a place to sleep. Knowing that was what I needed, I looked and looked but reported back to her that I couldn't find one I liked in my price range.

"You'll be sorry if you don't have a place for your friends to spend the night," she repeatedly told me. "I know you too well."

We finally agreed the answer was a trundle bed. Then we were both happy—I got the sofa I wanted and my friends also had a bed to sleep in. Then, much to my surprise, she gave me the money to buy the bed.

The next thing I needed, of course, was a dresser. "Would this one work?" Ethel asked pointing to an extra four-drawer dresser with bookcase. "Fantastic!" I replied, and she immediately set to work emptying the drawers.

Ethel always ate her meals on a tray in her favorite chair by the window. Her drop-leaf table and two swivel chairs were just a catch-all that she could get along without. Consequently, my dining room was now furnished.

I also inherited a green hurricane lamp which Ethel knew would go perfectly in my pink and green bedroom. However, as my friend Dave Anderson and I loaded the furniture into the van, we noticed my new possessions included a pink potty chair! She knew it was the right color for my bedroom. I frowned. It was an item I really didn't need, but I didn't have the heart to tell Ethel, so I gratefully accepted it.

The Bunker Hill doorman was curious as he saw us carrying out the furniture. I explained we were furnishing my new apartment.

"Can you use a TV set?" asked the man I had come to know through my frequent visits to the Towers.

"Sure could," I replied since the TV had been owned by my roommate. The next Saturday he brought me an old black and white portable, but part of the agreement was I was not to tell "Miss Waters." He didn't want to be rewarded by her for his good deed.

As Dave and I drove to Burbank to unload my new furnishings, I moaned that I didn't know what I was going to do with that pink potty. Dave, with his huge house and sense of imagination, said, "I'll take it."

"It's yours," I told him, wondering what in the world he was going to do with it. He was excited to have a possession of Ethel Waters's, and I'll have to admit it looked good in his den filled with a beautiful green plant.

Since decorating my apartment had been a joint effort, I

invited Ethel to have lunch with me one Saturday. I was anxious for her to see it, although I knew it was an effort for her to leave the comforts of her home.

Ethel preferred plain and simple foods, so I put aside my gourmet cooking and concocted a stew. She liked her food highly seasoned so I spiced it up the best I knew how, and it was a success.

I was nervous about this event. My apartment was full of objects she had given me, but I worried that she would notice the missing pieces.

She was thrilled at my new home. She went from room to room examining the place. "It's so homey," she said, "and decorated with real style."

"Yeah," I reminded her, "Waters style."

As we drove back to her apartment, she confessed to me she had second thoughts about coming. But she had told me she would come and didn't want to go back on her word. She was glad she had made the effort.

Ethel was silent for miles of the journey home which was not unusual. I realized she had been deep in thought when she said "Twila, where in your apartment would you hang that photograph of me that I said you could have?"

For years I had admired a black and white photo that hung above her piano. (It is reproduced as the frontispiece to this book.) She had promised that some day it would be mine.

I admitted I really didn't know.

"It belongs right above your sofa," she said. I gulped. I had not considered hanging it in the most prominent spot in my living room. She immediately sensed we were not thinking on the same level. So that cherished picture hung in her living room until she gave up her apartment. Even then, she gave it to me "on loan" with the understanding that she might ask for it back.

When Ethel learned that my real mom and dad were

going to visit me from Iowa, she announced that we were to be her guests for lunch. This was another rare occasion and a real treat for my parents, who were anxious to meet this lady I had written home about. The meeting of my two Moms was quite an occasion.

Ethel had seen The Sizzler advertised on TV and their steaks looked very tempting to her, so she decided that's where we'd eat. I chauffeured the four of us around Los Angeles looking for the closest one. As we were eating, I silently chuckled as Ethel nicknamed my dad "Silent Jim."

Before I took my parents on a sightseeing tour, we drove Ethel back home. As we were leaving her apartment, my dad noticed a huge train plaque on her wall, a gift from the Special Train Committee of Tennessee. He admired it and Ethel half-jokingly said, "Who knows, maybe some day you'll fall heir to that." Dad grinned, not knowing whether to take her seriously. Over a year later when she was forced to put her belongings into storage, she said to me, "You get that train off to your dad." I did immediately. When that package arrived in Iowa, Dad was probably the happiest man around.

As in any mother-daughter relationship, Ethel and I had our fights. She would often blame my stubbornness on my German background.

On my arrival one day, I was met at the door with the accusation of "really messing things up." She had received her bank statement and it didn't jibe with her checkbook. It was naturally my fault, since I wrote out most of her checks. It made her nervous filling in the blanks since her eyesight was so bad. It was one of those days that I didn't want to take criticism. I blurted out, "Of course, I make mistakes. I'm only human. I make mistakes in my own checkbook. Maybe you should get somebody else who can do the job better. I'm doing the best I can."

I was amazed at myself for letting off this steam. Evidently these thoughts were buried and today they were all surfacing.

Ethel told me to calm down. "We both know I can't get someone else," she said. "But maybe it isn't fair that you come every week. You call me and if I don't have something that's urgent, you wouldn't have to come every Saturday," she told me.

I left that day without the real problem being solved. Later I felt guilty about it. I should have had better control of the situation. After all she had nobody day after day, and these little things were important to her. I knew something could happen to her any day, and I would forever feel terrible if a day like that were our last memories together.

Days went by. I couldn't bring myself to phone and apologize. When I finally called, no mention was made of our squabble. The next Saturday I made my usual trek to see her. The air was cool but neither of us mentioned the incident. Gradually it was forgotten.

Weeks later I learned that I hadn't made the error in her checkbook. It was her tax man. He had written out her federal and state income tax checks. He entered them correctly in her book but had made both checks for the same amount. Several weeks later she received a refund from the state government and never mentioned it to me. Consequently, it was some time before we straightened out the matter.

However, she never apologized for blaming me for that error, nor did I ever mention it to her again.

Ethel did admit to having a short temper. She wrote in *To Me It's Wonderful:* "People can still hurt me. Jesus never will. I can hurt myself by acting too quick, jumping before I've stopped to listen to His still small voice! Shootin' off with that short tongue. I still do that and before I know it, I've ended up in the woodshed."

Not long after our disagreement, a couple of my friends and I were fortunate to get front row seats at a ladies' meeting where Ruth Graham was the speaker and Ethel the guest soloist. Over seven thousand ladies attended. Bill Brown escorted Ethel onto the platform and pointed out my special spot.

After several songs—Ethel said she didn't sing but recited musically—she closed with "His Eye Is on the Sparrow." She had sung it thousands of times—over five hundred times in *The Member of the Wedding*. People never tired of hearing her sing it.

> *I sing because I'm happy,*
> *I sing because I'm free.*
> *For His eye is on the sparrow,*
> *And I know . . .*

Wait. Here was a new line . . .

> *Mom knows, Twila,*
> *He watches me.*

Had I heard right? Did Ethel really add my name to her favorite hymn? Yes. I had heard right. World Wide Pictures's sound man, Les Kisling, recorded the entire program and gave me a cassette of that special song as a keepsake.

Another favorite keepsake I have from Ethel is a little red ginger jar. Former President Richard Nixon sent it to her from his historic 1972 visit to Red China. I always admired it. If I took anyone to Ethel's apartment, I would point out the little jar to them and give them a history lesson. When Ethel gave up her apartment she said to me, "Twila, I want you to have that because you loved it so much."

I never would have been able to ask her for it. I never could ask for anything she had. I knew how much she detested freeloaders, as she called them. There would be times I deliberately neglected telling her something for fear she would think I was asking for a favor.

About this time, Doug Oldham contacted me about the possibility of Ethel's appearing with him as a special guest on a new TV show he was hosting. He persuaded me by saying he would make it simple for Ethel by bringing the camera to her apartment, or renting a nearby studio or even taping in a park. It was her decision to do what was most convenient. Ethel would never allow anyone to come to her apartment, so when I told her the choices, she said, "Twila, why can't we do it at your place."

"Sure," I replied while in the back of my mind I was thinking about the cleaning, how small my apartment was, and how hot it could get in the summer.

The appointed Saturday I left my apartment unlocked so that Doug and his crew could set up, while I drove downtown to pick up the guest star. We came back to my place to find it jammed with lights, sound equipment and five men. Doug had thoughtfully brought roses for Ethel and me.

Ethel sat on my love seat and Doug on the ottoman. The microphone was turned on. Doug asked a question and Ethel was off rambling. When she knew she had a captive audience, she was a different person—the actress in her came out and she was "on stage." She went from one subject to another without letting Doug ask a question. As soon as the microphone was turned off, Ethel reverted to her "normal" relaxed self. If only there was a way to record her without her knowing it.

Then there was the time Ethel's agent called her to do a role in the "Owen Marshall" TV show. After she read the script and knew she could identify with the part, she agreed to do it, even though it had been years since she had done a dramatic part. She was told her part would only take several hours of shooting time.

I drove her to Universal Studios where we were met by the director and producer and shown to the stage. The lights were blazing, grips and set decorators were scurrying around adjusting last minute details. People from the wardrobe and make-up departments came by and were most helpful in seeing that Ethel had what she needed.

Ethel's scene was with Lee Majors, the blonde, blue-eyed co-star of the show. When the director called for a rehearsal on the set, Ethel was terribly frustrated with herself—she couldn't remember her lines. Time after time she would turn the lines around.

Finally the director yelled "cut." Ethel, Lee and I found a corner where we could help her with her lines. I had the copy of the script and was the prompter. Lee was very patient and understanding. Ethel tried so hard.

When Lee stepped away for a few moments, Ethel leaned over to me and whispered, "Twila, I can't concentrate when he's staring at me with those beautiful big blue eyes"!

"Everybody gets an Oscar with Jesus."

Chapter Six

Sixty years in show business! Ethel Waters had lots of honors and awards to show for it. The framed certificates that hung on the walls and the memorabilia around her apartment were proof of it. She never bragged about her accomplishments. To her they represented things of the past and now her life was different. "Everybody gets an Oscar with Jesus," was her view.

A reporter once asked her if she would ever make a comeback, "Oh, honey, that's a lost ball in the high weeds," she replied.

She did comment once that she was grateful Jesus had allowed her to give out what she felt inside. She had done that on the stage, and was doing it now in her sacred concerts. "When I sing 'Sparrow,' I know I'm the sparrow he's watched over all these years."

For fifteen years now Ethel had been singing in the Billy Graham Crusades. To express his gratitude to Ethel and to tell the movie industry of her love and faith in Jesus Christ, Billy Graham honored Ethel with a testimonial dinner on October 6, 1972.

That Friday evening, as the guests were arriving at the Century Plaza Hotel in their limousines, Joan Brown and I were in Ethel's suite pinning back her bra straps. We assured her she looked just beautiful as she stepped back to look at herself in the mirror. Her white hair was tucked in place under the little brown scarf which matched her caramel colored chiffon dress trimmed with brown lace. Only minutes before, she had realized that she didn't have an evening bag, and Joan had scurried to the stores just before closing time to purchase one.

Shopping for Ethel was not easy. I remembered how Joan and I had tried to buy Ethel a new evening dress for this special occasion. Fred Dienert had generously offered to foot the bill. We wanted the guest of honor to look stunning but her health was not up to a shopping spree. Joan and I were delegated the buyers, and we began hunting stores that carried dresses large enough for Ethel. Our choices were soon narrowed down to Lane Bryant in Beverly Hills.

We found a beautiful pink, elegant but simple Mr. Blackwell original, which we felt suited Ethel. However, the store refused to let us bring back the dress if it didn't meet with Ethel's approval. The saleslady agreed to let us use the phone to call Ethel and describe the dress to her. Ethel was indignant. "Pink is *not* my color," she bellowed at me, "and besides what are you doing at Lane Bryant? That's a store for *fat* people!" I meekly hung up the phone feeling defeated. Joan and I thanked the saleslady for her help and walked out.

Tonight Ethel looked very lovely in her dress which was made especially for her in the 1940s.

Joan and I escorted her downstairs to the Brentwood Room for a private reception where she could first greet selected VIPs. I was to meet my date there. Ethel had arranged for me to be escorted by the editor of her recently published book.

I was standing at the doorway as one of the special guests

arrived—Tricia Nixon Cox with her stoic secret service men. She looked like a fairy princess in her long white dress and blonde hair as she nodded a greeting to me. Ethel welcomed her with a bear hug and reminded her, "I haven't seen you since your wedding in the White House garden."

Ethel was hyped up for this big event as she greeted the other guests—Hugh Downs, Billy Daniels, Peter Lind Hayes and Jim Nabors.

The press and photographers were kept at a distance until ten minutes before the head table guests were to enter the grand ballroom. At the appointed time, all surged forward into the tiny room. Flash bulbs popped and TV lights blazed.

Billy Graham presented Ethel with an engraved silver tray reading, "With love and appreciation for 15 years of singing in our crusades." Two weeks later when Ethel learned I was entertaining guests in my home she gave me the silver tray. "You'll get more use out of it than I will. But don't let anyone from the Team know I gave it to you!"

As the picture-taking continued, one photographer mistakenly called her Mrs. Waters. "It's Miss," she chided him. "Don't spoil my chances."

Dr. Graham spoke to the press, "We're here to honor Ethel Waters. She made it in show business when it was difficult for a black actress to make it." She stopped him short. I cringed. I knew what was coming.

"Please, not that word *black*," she scolded him. "I'm a Negress and proud of it."

Previous experience had taught me that to her black was just a color. "Nobody in our race is jet black," she had told me. "I'm a brown-skinned woman. The term *black* came into being with the militants." Once she had even told a reporter, "You can call me a Negro or Negress, but if you call me a Nigger, I'm gonna slap you across the face even though I'm a Christian."

Ethel and I at the St. Louis Crusade where I was her esc[ort].
Below: The Melvin Knaacks, my parents, and Ethel. T[he]
meeting of my two Moms was a real occasion. (*Russ Bu*[sby]
photo.)

ginald Beane was Ethel's accompa-
t for many years.

Ruth Graham, Ethel, and Mary Crowley in Dallas, Sept. 1971. *(Bob Kornegay
photo.)*

Ethel and Cy Jackson

Jarrell McCracken and Ethel
(Windy Drum photo)

In the 50s and 60s
Ethel gave performances
of her one-woman show,
An Evening with Ethel Waters,
all over the country.

Ethel at the 1971 testimonial dinner given for her in Los Angeles by the Billy Graham Association. Left above: With Julie Harris. Below: Billy Graham presents Ethel with an engraved silver tray while Tricia Nixon Cox and Ruth Graham enjoy the moment. (*Russ Busby photos.*)

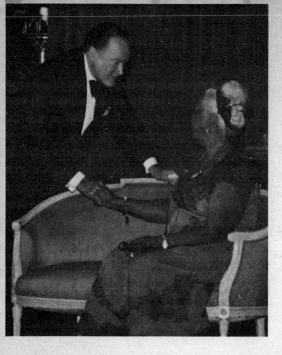

Bob Hope greets Ethel at the testimonial dinner.

Bill and Joan Brown with Ethel at the dinner. (*Russ Busby photos.*)

Ethel loved singing at the Graham crusades. The top two pictures show her in 1957, weighing over 350 lbs. Bill Brown (top right) had to take an arm off a chair for her. Bottom left: Cliff Barrows was one of her precious children.

Right: Ethel at her last crusade, San Diego, August 1976.

(All except top two Russ Busby photos.)

Left: Ethel in the dress I made for her out of the lining of an old raincoat.

With her boisterous enthusiasm, Ethel continued her speech with "I'm proud of being an American." She then turned to Tricia and said, "I love your dad and I love the world."

On that upbeat, everyone filed into the ballroom to join the more than nine hundred guests. The celebrity list was impressive and included people Ethel had worked with and others who simply admired her—the Gene Autrys, Bob and Rosemary Stack, Red Buttons, Jack Oakie, Joanne Carson, George Maharis, Mrs. Clark Gable, the Don De Fores, Robert Young—and Christian leaders such as Campus Crusade director Bill Bright and World Vision president Stan Mooneyham.

Jim Nabors's baritone voice rang out with the national anthem, the invocation was given by Dr. E. V. Hill and then the sound of silverware as the crowd began to devour their meal of roast sirloin of beef.

I had been caught up in the activities of the day and was almost too excited to eat. It was almost as though I was feeling every emotion with Ethel. I kept one eye focused on her the entire evening, trying to read her penetrating eyes and that somber look. It was a tense time for me. At every exuberant laugh that burst forth from her, I could relax a little.

Hugh Downs, the master of ceremonies, began the evening's program with "We're meeting here to honor a great lady. Every one of us is aware of the place she has established for herself in the annals of show business through all media —vaudeville, clubs, Broadway, radio, films and television. She has become a part of every one of our lives. The honor is ours—just for the privilege of knowing her and having her as part of our lives."

We could hardly see the doll-like figure of Tricia Cox as she stepped to the podium to read her speech: "It's really a special pleasure for me to be with you this evening to help honor a great American artist who has been beloved by so many Americans for so long and who has also been such a wonderful friend of the Nixon family. That friendship, as a matter of fact, is now in its third generation with no generation gap in sight." Ethel loved that and so did the audience.

Tricia continued with a telegram from her father, Richard Nixon, telling how Ethel had touched the hearts of Americans with her magnetic and majestic voice.

Nixon had also prepared a tape for the program. Ethel's eyes were misty as she heard the President say, "We think of her as practically a member of our family. She brought that family feeling with her when she performed at the White House. She brings it to every group she is with, wherever she goes. As Billy Graham knows, it is one thing to sing the gospel, it is another thing to live the gospel, but Ethel Waters does both with as much spirit as anyone I know. Ethel, we love you, we thank you, we wish you many more years of happiness and success."

Another special guest for the evening was Bob Hope. As usual, his monologue was crammed with jokes. "I knew Billy Graham had something to do with this dinner when I saw the catering truck unload five loaves and two fishes.

"Ethel sings so beautifully," Bob continued, "that one time at an outdoor concert, a pair of canaries swooped to her shoulder and whispered, 'Cool it, you're spoiling our act.' "

His one-liners included "They used to call her Sweet Mama Stringbean. She was the Twiggy of her day," and "She has brought more happiness to people than tax refunds."

He concluded with "You have had your share of 'Stormy Weather' and have weathered many 'Heat Waves!' I hope you walk in many green pastures before you reach your 'Cabin in the Sky.' "

Singer Billy Daniels was next. He used the opportunity while he had the microphone in hand, to sing number after number. Then, even though the hour was getting late, he had one more song he wanted to sing for Ethel. I recognized that scowl on her face as she mumbled to him, "I don't think you have time," and looked around for someone to confirm her statement. No one did. He sang "Old Black Magic," much to her dismay.

Hugh Downs introduced Julie Harris who joined Ethel on the center stage. There were "ohs," "mys" and laughter from Ethel, since she didn't know her darling girl Julie was in the audience.

Julie handed Ethel a long-stem red rose and blinked back tears as she reminisced about their working together in *The Member of the Wedding* at the Empire Theatre in New York City. Julie, with her delicate voice, remembered when Ethel took her curtain calls that it "sounded like thunder." She said, "I was the one who got to sit on Ethel's lap every night and it was heaven on earth. I love her with all my heart."

Ethel had fond memories of working with Julie. She recalled, "I would have to squeeze Julie at the end of the song, 'His Eye Is on the Sparrow,' as she would completely go to sleep on my lap. So I would nudge her so she could come in on her part."

Next on the program was Los Angeles County Supervisor Kenneth Hahn with a proclamation that cited Ethel as "one of America's outstanding citizens."

"Wow!" was Ethel's only comment.

I was proud of Ethel—proud that she was my Mom and not just a "superstar" to me.

Ethel was overwhelmed with all the love and admiration she received in one evening.

It was Billy Graham's turn to speak next. "I have learned through the years that when it reaches 11:00 P.M. not to preach." However, he continued, "I have learned a lot of things from Ethel Waters. She is a woman of determination. She is a lady with a sense of humor. She is also a woman of humility, a woman of discernment." He went on to tell about her compassion and the countless people to whom she had given of her time and money to help. "She's a woman of God. Some of the greatest philosophy and theology I have heard anywhere in the world has come from her lips and heart and mind. I have often wished I had her spontaneous gift of thought. She comes out with such brilliant things that later, though I don't suppose she knew it, I have turned around and used them in my sermons."

I really doubted that Ethel didn't know it. No one outwitted her.

At last the guest of honor had her chance to speak. "I'm suppose to be lookin' glamorous. I hope I look all right," she worried aloud. That was followed by her whoop of laughter.

She admitted she rambled, but added, "You have that privilege when you are old.

"You don't go to heaven in a group. You have to go the straight and narrow gate. You have to get it right before you leave here. When the Lord comes into your life, you know it. God was so patient with me. I ain't gonna turn Him loose now," she preached. Then she eased into singing "Partners with God."

Billy Graham presented her with a book of photographs of famous people and said, "God bless you for a wonderful evening we will never forget. We are going to see you for many years here on earth, but we also are going to spend eternity with you in heaven."

The evening was not complete. Ethel hadn't sung "His Eye Is on the Sparrow" yet. With fire in her eyes, she demanded orchestra conductor Ralph Carmichael not to "swing" with her song but to do it her way. He did. She gave the audience what they were waiting for. Even though the hour was late the guests all stayed to join her on the last chorus.

Ethel was weary but keyed up as she sat on the aqua love

seat greeting guests until long past midnight. Then, beat but still on cloud nine from the evening activities, she asked me if I would spend the night with her. She had been given a beautiful suite for the night and she wanted to share it with me.

Ethel warned me as she climbed into bed, "If I start snoring, just wake me up and I'll turn over." Within minutes that dreadful noise penetrated the room. I just didn't have the heart to wake up the exhausted lady. I suffered through the night without sleeping a wink, eagerly waiting until I could go home and get some rest.

Ethel received other honors, including recognition from her hometown, Chester, Pennsylvania, where they held a parade and named a park in her honor.

On one of my Saturday visits with Ethel, she told me that MGM was going to include a segment of her performance in *Cabin in the Sky* in their new film, *That's Entertainment, Part II*. She always saved the good news until she saw me in person. I think she liked to see my excitement.

However, I was in Honolulu when she received the news that Mike Douglas wanted her on his show as he saluted the cast of *That's Entertainment, II*. Her decision to accept the invitation depended on whether I would be back in Los Angeles to attend with her.

My boss called me to present the assignment. Not one to miss a party, I agreed to arrive home the day of the big affair.

From Ethel's place we were chauffeured in a limousine to the MGM lot for the taping of the show. A soundstage had been decorated as a park with flowers everywhere, park benches, and fresh fruit stands. People were wandering around eating salmon, French bread and cheese, while Mike Douglas interviewed the hosts of the forthcoming film—Gene Kelly and Fred Astaire. It was noisy on the set and I was amazed they could tape with all the activity. Ethel and I took a seat. George Burns came by to say hello. Tony Bennett introduced himself. I was loving every minute.

After Nanette Fabray had done a dance number with Debbie Reynolds, it was Ethel's turn to be interviewed. I seized the opportunity to snoop around as Ethel was helped to the center stage. There was lots of chatter as I wandered and nibbled on the bread and cheese.

Suddenly a hush went over the stage and I crowded forward to see what I was missing. Ethel and Mike were singing "Cabin in the Sky." He let her finish as she talked and sang that old song. It was a magical moment.

The next day the Hollywood Reporter said of the incident, "There was hardly a dry eye in the room when Ethel Waters sang." She still commanded respect from her show business friends.

In May of that year she received her invitation to attend the premiere showing of That's Entertainment, II. Once again she depended on me to go along with her. Knowing she was my "ticket" to these gala events, I seized every opportunity to go.

With the gold tickets in my hand, Ethel and I relaxed in the limousine on our way to the Cinerama Dome Theatre. A block from the theatre we were to transfer to vintage cars that would take us to the theatre's entrance.

I climbed into the back seat of the 1952 brown Hudson convertible. Ethel was up front with the driver.

As we rounded the corner, we saw the crowd that had gathered to watch the celebrities arrive. The car moved slowly as we waved at the cheering fans.

One lady gasped and said, "Oh, look, there's Ethel . . . Merman." I panicked in the back seat. I knew how Ethel hated to be mistaken for another celebrity. There was silence for what seemed like eternity. Finally she turned to me and said, "She must have been looking at you. At least you're the right color."

The driver stopped the car in front of the theatre. Ruth Ashton Taylor stepped forward and asked for an interview. However, it was seven minutes until air time, and since her program was "live," she asked if we could possibly go around the block one more time.

We did. Ethel joked with the young driver about his having to go "the extra mile."

The crowd was confused as we rounded the corner again, but the timing was right. Ms. Taylor got her interview.

The parking lot was transformed for a "picnic in the patio." Food stalls were serving quiche Lorraine, roast beef, lasagne, tacos and fancy desserts. I made the rounds heaping my plate, but Ethel refused to indulge.

Just before 8:00 P.M. we made our way into the theatre to find seats F2 and F4. Since Ethel's eyesight was so poor, I would often whisper the names of people who stopped to chat with her, though I was of little help around show business people. I did recognize Groucho Marx and whispered his name to Ethel before he shuffled to us to say "hello." "Thanks for telling me," she whispered back. "It's been so long since I've seen him."

That's Entertainment, II came alive for me as I sat between Ethel Waters and FiFi D'Orsay, ladies who represented two segments of that great film. FiFi nudged me and told me the history and story of each old film clip as it appeared on the screen.

In May 1976, Bill Brown and I planned a gathering of Ethel's closest friends to show Cabin in the Sky. Ethel was the happiest when she was around people who loved her for herself and not her name.

That evening as the lights went out and the curtain went up, I could tell Ethel was so proud that her "family" was going to view her performance in this all Negro movie made in 1943. It also starred Lena Horne, Louis Armstrong, Eddie

("Rochester") Anderson and Butterfly McQueen. "I'm the only big name in that film," Ethel had boasted.

I had only seen Ethel in one other movie—*The Member of the Wedding*. I was amazed at the shimmying and shaking she could do—so different from the Ethel Waters I knew.

As I served refreshments to the group after the movie, Ethel beckoned me to come to her side, "Twila," she said, "you've worked hard on organizing this evening. I know you're tired. I think I can get along without your coming to my place tomorrow."

"Wow," I thought to myself, "a Saturday to sleep late."

But I never got that chance to sleep in. The phone rang early in the morning. It was Ethel.

"Twi, I just want to thank you again for last night. It was such a beautiful gesture." In real sincerity she continued, "That was the first time somebody has done something for me where I wasn't expected to give something in return."

"I might only be able to croak, but this sparrow wants to be heard."

Chapter Seven

"BALLS, PICNICS AND FESTIVALS," Ethel exclaimed as she pried herself from my little white Datsun 240Z. She had asked when she was going to get a ride in my new sports car, and this trip to the airport was her first experience.

"Nothin' like exposing my southern hemisphere," she muttered as the colored porter helped her out.

I laughed. What a good sport she was at seventy-eight!

Ethel Waters was on her way to sing at another Billy Graham Crusade. She saved every ounce of strength she could so that whenever and wherever Cliff Barrows asked her to go, she would be ready. Deep down she believed she was the "big draw" at the crusades. She didn't like music with a beat and didn't like the way the younger generation was "swinging" with gospel music. They were doing rock music—not Christian music. She didn't like churches or so called "Christian organizations" where "Jesus went through on stilts." She believed in the straightforward gospel message.

I kissed her goodbye and said, "I love you."

"I know it," she replied. Then the porter whisked her off in a wheelchair with her luggage piled on her lap. She never trusted the airlines to check her baggage through to her destination.

As I drove away from the airport I wondered if she would return alive. She had so many physical problems that she was a walking miracle.

I remembered back to the time I discovered that her lunch that day had been a package of doughnuts. "I don't have the strength to stand in my kitchen and fix a salad," she had told me. "I'm not steady with a knife and I'm afraid of cutting myself."

It was no wonder she was getting weak from that kind of diet.

In order to get the proper care she needed, I finally talked her into staying at a convalescent hospital, although it meant she would be sidelined from several crusades. One near my office met with her approval.

I helped her pack her bags. From her safety deposit box in the bank, she took out travelers checks dating back to the 1950s which would pay for her three-month stay. At the hospital she settled into a tiny private room.

Some doctors and nurses were immediately adopted into her "family"; others she only grunted at when they entered her room. Her "babies" were rewarded with a copy of *To Me It's Wonderful,* her second book published in 1972, and those who were extra special were given a bonus of her "Sparrow" album. Many of the nurses, though, she felt only came into her room because they wanted a chance to see and meet Ethel Waters. Their concern for her well-being was taken as an annoyance.

Ethel demanded privacy. When one elderly gentleman resident entered her room by mistake looking for his own room, she was extremely upset over the intrusion.

She phoned me at my office, "Twi, I have a favor to ask of you. Now don't you dare laugh," she begged me. I couldn't imagine what it was she needed.

"I want you to bring me a broom handle so I can poke people who have no business comin' in my room," she said. I couldn't help laughing as I pictured this scene, but Ethel was serious.

I went to our maintenance man at the studio for help. "John, where am I going to get a long stick?" I asked. He found a long dowel for me and made sure it had a rounded end.

My next problem was how to get it into her hospital room. However, the old adage, "If you act like you know what you're doing, no one will question you," worked for me. I walked down the long hospital corridor to her room as if I always carried a stick. No one stopped me. Once again Ethel was glad she could count on me.

Thank goodness she never attempted to use that stick, but it soothed her mind knowing it was by her side.

By choice, Ethel had few visitors during this hospital stay. "Don't tell people where I am," she insisted. It wasn't always easy to tell her friends she didn't want to be bothered. Every day on lunch hour I would stop by to let her know I cared. Often I would have to run down to the Bunker Hill Towers to get books, albums, her mail, or forgotten items she thought she needed. I would sometimes stop at a grocery store to buy her crackers or fruit when she complained about the meals. Even though the time I spent with her seemed a handicap to my independent nature, I took the responsibility seriously.

One day she asked Bill and Joan Brown if they would buy a wedding gift for a special friend of hers. "Twila is too scatterbrained to do it," she told Bill. When I first heard her description of me I thought it was humorous. But the more I thought about it the more it hurt—my best wasn't good enough.

Ethel never liked it when her bullheadedness was challenged by someone. Bill Brown recalls an incident when he and Cliff Barrows visited Ethel in the convalescent home.

A couple of nights before, Ethel had fallen while walking to the bathroom. I suggested she get one of those aluminum walkers older people hold in front of them to steady them for each step. Ethel's pride caused her to reject my suggestion and with a sanctimonious tone, she replied, "I don't need no walker. The Lord is here to guide my footsteps." When I asked her where her Lord was the night she had fallen, she gave no answer. Smiling I repeated the question. "Where was your Lord when you fell?"

"I heard you the first time, you little snip," she retorted.

The rest and good food Ethel received at the convalescent home put her back on her feet, and she was able to go back to her apartment at the Bunker Hill Towers. Through one of her nurses, she found a maid to come by daily and help with the cooking and cleaning. Ethel thanked the good Lord that He had provided her with a place to recuperate but rejoiced even more at being able to go back home.

Shortly after she returned home she had an ophthalmologist check her blurred vision. He confirmed that she had cataracts on both eyes—a result of uncontrolled diabetes.

So it was back to a hospital—Hollywood Presbyterian—for cataract surgery. She demanded no publicity or fanfare as she checked in. The surgery went smoothly and Ethel picked and chose new friends among the doctors and nurses during her three-day stay.

Eager to be on her way home, Ethel had her overnight bag on her lap as a nurse pushed Ethel's wheelchair down the corridor and into the elevator. I walked along beside. "This is my baby girl," Ethel chirped to the nurse. Another passenger on the elevator looked at Ethel Waters and then at me. Even though Ethel had just come through eye surgery she didn't miss that passenger's quizzical look. "By proxy, of course," she added and let out one of her hearty whoops of laughter.

Ethel had missed several crusades because of her poor health. She was excited as a child with a new toy when Cliff Barrows asked her if she was up to singing at the St. Louis crusade. Knowing her health was still a little shaky, I was asked to accompany her. Ethel was glad to have a travel companion, and I was glad for the opportunity to see old crusade friends again.

With first-class tickets in hand, we were dropped off at the Los Angeles airport. The porters, as usual, were glad to see Ethel—not only because of the generous tips she gave them ("They expect it of me," she said) but because they genuinely loved her. She always had a kiss and hug for each one.

It was a privilege for the porters to get her to the right gate and put her on the plane before the other passengers. She preferred a particular seat—second row, aisle seat, right hand side—which I automatically learned to request when making reservations.

Passengers on the plane would often recognize her as they boarded and would whisper to their friends, "Look . . . there's Ethel Waters!" Some would recognize her but couldn't think of her name. It would be a bumpy ride if someone mistakenly called her Mahalia Jackson or dared to ask her name. Some just had to touch her. Others would say "I'll never forget your performance in *Member of the Wedding*—or *Cabin in the Sky*." I would burst with pride as I heard the accolades given her.

It was not unusual for a stewardess to come by and ask to take a picture for a shy passenger or request an autograph. Since her eyesight had failed, Ethel refused to oblige, as it was a struggle for her to sign her name. If she did it for one person she would have to do it for all.

On that first flight with Ethel, she reminisced of the time years ago when she was too fat to get a seatbelt around her. She had asked the stewardess for an extension for the belt, but there was none on board. The stewardess went to the cockpit to tell the pilot the problem. He told the stewardess to assure Ethel he would do his best at an easy take-off and landing. "And that's the truth," she exclaimed as we both roared over the incident.

As we checked into our hotel in St. Louis, we discovered a mix-up on our connecting rooms. The only way they could accommodate us was two single rooms on different floors or one big double room.

Those huge brown eyes of Ethel's pierced my soul as she said, "Oh, Twi, we could share, couldn't we?" That pleading look got to me. I agreed, although I remembered that dreadful night I spent with her at the Century Plaza suite and didn't sleep a wink. Her snoring was still vivid in my memory. Then too, I wished I had brought along a flannel nightgown. She insisted on keeping her room so cool. "I have to because of my heart," she half apologized.

As we settled into our room, she said, "You can't imagine the loneliness of being confined to the four walls of a hotel room. People can love you from a distance," she said. She went on to tell me how night after night people expressed their love and appreciation for her acting performance in a Broadway show. When the curtain calls were over, she would hail a cab and go back to her hotel room alone. "One time I received seventeen curtain calls," she laughed as she said, "and the rope puller collapsed from exhaustion." Yet that night there was no one waiting to love her, the Ethel Waters who needed to be loved for herself. "I cried myself to sleep that night," she recollected.

I was glad I had agreed to share that room with her. Selfishly I still wondered how I was going to sleep while she snored.

Just knowing I was close at hand was good enough for Ethel. "You don't have to stay with me all the time," she remarked as she turned on the TV set. I excused myself to wait in the lobby for crusade friends.

Tedd Smith came in, and I casually mentioned my problem to him. He, in turn, told Grady Wilson my story. "I have some sleeping pills and ear plugs," Dr. Wilson said as he took off for his room.

He returned to the lobby with two sleeping tablets, one ear plug and a pencil eraser for the other plug. He had lost the other plug down the sink drain while sterilizing it with Listerine! However, I thanked God for friends and favors as I got a peaceful night of sleep.

The St. Louis audience enthusiastically welcomed Ethel to their crusade. She was glad to sing again about the Jesus she loved so much. She received four standing ovations, but because of her bad eyesight was completely unaware of it until I told her on our way back to the hotel.

"Did I sound okay? Did I say the right things?" she questioned me as we left the arena that night. "I never plan what I'm gonna say," she continued. I was surprised at the seemingly contradictory attitude of the woman who always displayed confidence.

I assured her she was as great as ever. The people had loved her. That's what she needed to hear.

On the plane coming back to Los Angeles, we sat behind a prominent actor. Ethel immediately recognized him for his television roles. She complimented him on his masterful acting ability.

This show business guy was intrigued by Ethel. He kept turning around in his seat asking her questions. "What were you doing in St. Louis? Have you written any books recently? Have you made any new albums?"

Ethel told him about her book recently published. She assured him I would see that he got an autographed copy along with several of her albums.

Several times I called the handsome bachelor to work out a time and place to deliver the goods. He called me several times, but we just couldn't get our schedules to coincide.

Ethel learned through the grapevine that this actor had shown a special interest in me. Over the phone one morning she confronted me with the matter. With her quick sense of humor, she said, "Twila, he's too old for you. I could see that with my cataracts. You shoulda been able to see that with your contacts!"

Although her physical limitations made it difficult for her to do the things she once did, the wit and wisdom of Waters was as sharp as ever, and she could laugh at herself. "When I feel myself gettin' short of breath," she once said, "I just keep my big fat mouth shut until I gather some more breath."

I remember at a crusade in Pittsburgh, when Ethel got to the podium to sing, she was laughing with gusto.

Goodness! What's with her? I wondered. Then she explained.

Usually the person sitting next to her on the platform would say, "Holding you up in prayer," when it came time for her to sing. However, just as she got up, Grady Wilson leaned over and said, "Your slip is showing."

"I'm the Christian Phyllis Diller," she said as the packed stadium joined with her in laughter.

As Ethel and I flew to attend the crusade in Albuquerque, she told me of her last visit to this city. She had come to the city by train to do a secular concert. This time she was coming to tell the people about her precious Savior.

We landed at the airport and began our descent from the airplane before I noticed the two parked cars on the runway. It must be an emergency, I thought, watching the flashing red light on the police car.

Then I spotted Larry Turner, the crusade associate. He was waiting for us at the bottom of the stairs. This was our official welcome to Albuquerque. Larry had arranged for us to step into the waiting car and be whisked off the runway without ever stepping foot in the terminal. Maybe Ethel was accustomed to such VIP treatment. It was a first for me.

"Hi," Ethel would exclaim with a burst of enthusiasm as she greeted the crusade crowd. The Ethel Waters I saw in front of a microphone was a totally different person from the one I saw behind the scenes.

I saw the one who was unsteady on her feet, the lady who stayed in bed all day long to have the strength to walk to the platform. I knew the woman who endured countless pains to be a part of a crusade. It would take her hours to get dressed because she needed to rest between each act of putting on her clothes. Her shoes went on last because often her feet were swollen.

For those few moments before the masses of people, God would grant her boundless energy, a twinkle for her eyes and a grin that stretched from ear to ear and showed the gap between her two front teeth. Her face glowed with God's love when she could talk about her Jesus.

People would come up to Ethel and tell her she was looking better than ever. As they would walk away, she would whisper to me, "Twila, if they only knew how I felt." She hid every pain and never complained.

"Cliffie, my precious son, says, 'Take your time but keep it moving,' " Ethel would tell the crowd and then chuckle as if she had told the whole world Cliff Barrows's secret.

She liked to share God's goodness to her before she sang. Her songs were familiar—"Partners with God," which she coauthored, "To Me It's Wonderful," "I Do, Don't You," "Just A Closer Walk with Thee." But the one the people always wanted to hear was "His Eye Is on the Sparrow" which she did so beautifully with the crusade choir.

Often at the end of the song, she might add, to the beat of the music, "One more time, Teddy, so they get the message," as she sang the last several lines again.

Tedd Smith, who accompanied Ethel at the Billy Graham

Crusades from 1957 to 1976, remembers what it was like to play the piano for her:

Ethel always demanded that her accompaniments be played exactly as they were arranged. As long as she heard this, things were fine. If you ever digressed from what was written, watch out!

It was a usual sight to see Ethel squeezing my arm to steady herself as we walked to the hotel coffee shop. It annoyed Ethel as she tried to eat and strangers would come by and pose with her as a friend took a picture.

Often we found it easier to order room service. I would slowly read the menu to her and let her choose whatever she wanted. Then I would phone in the order. After I finished reading the menu to her in our room in Jackson, Mississippi, she insisted I order first. "Twi, you always wait until after I order and then you get something that looks so much better than mine." From then on, I ordered first and she would get the same thing.

As I traveled with Ethel, I noticed it becoming harder and harder for her to make the effort to get ready for a crusade. She wasn't about to let anybody know, though, as being at a crusade was what was keeping her going. "I might be only able to croak, but this sparrow wants to be heard," she once said.

"Oh, I'm gonna make a sexy corpse," she would tell photographer Russ Busby at every crusade as time after time he captured her famous smile on film.

In the summer of 1976 Cliff Barrows asked Ethel if she was physically able to journey to San Diego in August and sing two nights at the crusade. "I'll be there," she replied. Even if it took her last breath doing so, Ethel said her main objective in life was to please the Savior.

As I sat in the audience that last night in San Diego, I was amazed at her spunk and sparkle, knowing the pain she was enduring. This gifted woman could generate magic to the audience. I emphasized to her how the people loved her as I helped her from the platform to the waiting car.

I don't know if it was a premonition or her woman's intuition, but I remember her telling Lowell Jackson, a staff worker, as he stood by the car, "Well, this is probably my last crusade. So I'll be looking for ya in heaven."

"Now you children listen to Mom. If I was sitting over there I would smack you one, and then put my arms around you and love you real good."

Chapter Eight

ETHEL WOULD OFTEN SAY after hearing a Christian recording artist sing, "They're copying my style. The timing is the way I would do that song." According to Ethel, there were very few Christian singers who were pros.

Bill and Gloria Gaither were probably Ethel's favorite musicians. She didn't often listen to records—in fact, there were many unopened albums in the rack under her old portable stereo—but her two Gaither albums were almost worn out. She would sit by her window and sing along to the tunes of "Get All Excited" and "There's Something about That Name."

This is what Gloria Gaither said about their friendship with Ethel Waters:

Ethel Waters touched countless lives. Bill's and mine were only two of them. There are many people who have talent, there are lots of folks with special skills and abilities. But I am convinced that God doesn't need another good singer. He does need great souls who just may happen to also sing. God doesn't need another great doctor or preacher or orator or statesman. He does need some great souls, thoroughly committed to Him, who just happen to also be skillful at the healing arts, preaching sermons, moving audiences, or formulating laws.

Ethel Waters was more than a great performer, sensational singer, skillful communicator—she was a great soul. And the compassion of her heart came through her voice, and her words, and her performances to touch people, soul to soul, intimately, because we who heard her somehow knew she had hurt where we hurt; she had known pain and struggle and joy and victory as we knew them. She knew Jesus and it was His ability to touch people at the core of their being that we felt when we heard her.

She had so much to teach us who were young and not nearly so wise. I remember one night she attended one of our concerts in Los Angeles. We talked with her during the intermission as she sat backstage and felt at once elevated by her warmth and compassion, yet dwarfed by her grace and wisdom. During the second half she came out to do a chorus of our song, "He Touched Me" and then sang her famous trademark, "His Eye Is on the Sparrow." The moment her low alto voice began, a hush fell over the audience. In the four minutes it took her to communicate the song, it was as if her great spirit had reached into each seat to lovingly single out each man, woman and child and say to each, "This is for you. God's care is for you."

When she finished, the great crowd stood to their feet. The applause went on and on. They had felt God's love and needed to respond. She knew they needed to. Yet she knew too when that fine line was crossed between responding to a deep gratitude to God and praising the one who only communicated His message. When the crowd's applause turned to her as a human vessel, she graciously left the stage, leaving only Jesus to be praised.

Cliff Barrows, who extended the invitation for Ethel to

sing at Billy Graham Crusades around the world has fond memories of one appearance in particular:

In Knoxville, Tennessee, at one service she appeared with President Nixon and Billy. The stadium was filled to overflowing with 25,000 outside the gates, which gave a total of over 100,000 at the service that night. In the crowd there were about 156 people who were there to demonstrate and protest against the President and the war, and of course, there was a "running feud" going on prior to the service beginning with their chanting and the choir responding. We had 6,000 in the choir and although they could be heard easily, it was amazing to me how well the 156 could be heard who were sitting down on the thirty-yard line on the far side of the field. During the earlier part of the service they would interrupt on occasion with their chants, slogans, etc., and several times it reached a point when the ushers and even the Tennessee football team were ready to throw them out.

It was at one of these times that Ethel stood up, and in her very candid, pointed, and yet warm way chided them: "Now you children, listen to Mom. If I was sitting over there I would smack you one, and then put my arms around you and love you real good."

At this the whole place broke up, first in laughter and then applause, and she really got to them as she sang. Interestingly, following her solo, they quieted down considerably; in fact, after Billy started preaching, we didn't hear from them again. Some of them got up and left. Others remained the entire service, and at the invitation a few of those responded to receive Christ.

Ethel really had the audience in the palm of her hand and she could talk to them at any length about any subject. Won't heaven be wonderful, when we can sit and listen to her as long as she wants to talk and sing to us?

If Ethel Waters once touched your life, you never forgot it

as illustrated by this letter written to the *Los Angeles Times* by Eugene C. Washington:

As long as I live I'll never forget Ethel Waters and I'll never forget the time I first met her as a child in New York City.

I must have been about 9 years old, and late one night outside of a night spot on Sugar Hill, called the Fat Man, near the Polo Grounds, I was selling the New York Daily News, 2 cents a copy then, and just as I was about to go inside a lady stopped me and said with a smile, "Little boy, you can't come in here, you are too young and besides, why aren't you home in bed?"

I said to her, "I'm selling my newspapers and there is no one out here to buy them. Please let me stand here in the doorway." She then asked me how many papers I had left. I told her only five more. She then said, "Young man, here is 50 cents for the five copies. Now you take this and scat and go straight home to your mother."

That lady, I learned later that night from my mother, was Ethel Waters. Thank you again, Ethel Waters. May you rest in peace.

Jarrell McCracken, president of Word, Inc., shares his memories of the singer who made three albums—*His Eye Is on the Sparrow, Ethel Waters Reminisces* and *Just a Little Talk with Ethel*—for his company.

When I first met Ethel Waters I was struck by her captivating presence. She was an obviously happy person. Her zest for life permeated the attitude of everyone within range. To those who knew her and those who didn't, she was a terrific witness to what can happen within a person who has clearly made peace with God.

Beyond spreading joy and happiness, Ethel also imparted wisdom. She was very bright and agile mentally. If you en-

The Later Years

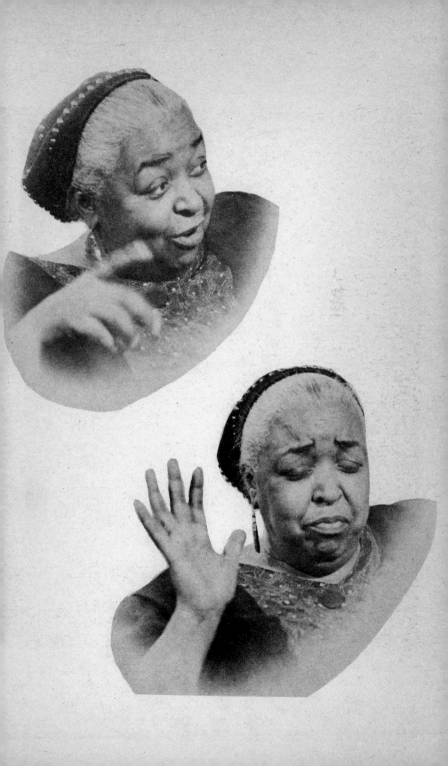

gaged in a battle of wits with Ethel you were sure to lose. She once said to a group of us, "I used to be little and cute. Now I'm fat and clever."

In her final days of illness and weakness, her faith was fervent and strong. There was still a beautiful spirit. Like always, I was a better person for having been with her in person or by phone.

Carol Kilpatrick, production manager for Word, recalls Ethel's coming to Waco for the open house of Word's new building in 1969.

My husband Pat went to Dallas to pick Ethel up at the airport. She was coming with Bill Carle, another of our recording artists. When she stepped off the plane, she was carrying a long leather strap—her seat belt extension! Pat put Bill Carle on the left side in the back seat. Although Bill was a pretty good size, when Ethel got in the front, Pat could see the station wagon kind of settle under the strain. For at least half of the ninety miles back to Waco, Bill complained about being in the back while Ethel sat in the front. Finally Ethel couldn't stand it any longer. She turned to Bill and said, "Bill, I've been praying all this time that you'd see the light and shut up. Now hush, child."

When they got to Waco, Ethel sat down on a new chair in the lobby, only to have it break under her. In a kind of prayer she exclaimed, "O Jesus, I done broke this chair too!"

Tedd Smith, pianist for the Billy Graham Crusades, has this to say about Ethel:

She was always her own person, no matter the circumstances. I can remember doing a concert with her one Sunday morning in the White House, Washington, D.C. It was during the Nixon administration, and there were approximately three hundred fifty government officials, Supreme Court justices and the presidential family gathered for the program. When I walked into the room, I was aware of the total silence, a sort of tomblike atmosphere. Ethel was introduced and she went to the microphone and immediately said, "Hi." The whole room seemed rather stunned by the informality and they greeted her with silence. Undaunted, Ethel grabbed the microphone, got in close to it and said, "I said hi!" Suddenly, the silence turned to laughter and the audience all shouted back "Hi!" Ethel turned the entire White House into one big family that morning and completely won their hearts.

She obviously grew up with the slogan "The show must go on," no matter how you felt. I can remember going to Ethel's room one night just before we were to do a concert in Montreat, North Carolina. She said, "I'm sick. I just won't be able to do the concert." I told her she would be all right and then went ahead to make certain the arrangements were in order at the auditorium. Fifteen minutes before the concert was to begin, an ambulance pulled up to the door and there was Ethel on a stretcher and an oxygen tank beside her. I thought, "She wasn't kidding. There is no way she can do this program." At eight o'clock, we heard a man say from the stage, "Ladies and gentlemen, Miss Ethel Waters." Suddenly she bounded from that stretcher and went on the platform to do an hour and a half program that was tremendous.

I loved Ethel Waters. Here was a woman who knew what human suffering was. Yet, she had also found answers to cope with the misery she had lived with since her birth. It was always a learning experience being with Ethel. She was strong-willed, definite about what she wanted, a thoroughly professional woman whose life influenced numbers of actors and singers and pointed the way to the One she loved so much. My life is sadder without her.

Dave Barr, a representative of World Wide Pictures, traveled with Ethel in 1959 promoting *The Heart is a Rebel*, a film Ethel made for World Wide Pictures. Dave told me about one incident that stands out in his memories:

The many enjoyable hours spent with Ethel as we traveled together for the premieres of The Heart Is a Rebel *could be all bottled up in one experience. At the film's premiere in Toronto, Canada, with 3,000 people in Massey Hall, Miss Waters requested an oversized chair for her platform appearance. Since she weighed 350 pounds at the time, this created some real problems. When we walked on stage and I was introducing Ethel to the people, it dawned on me that we had forgotten the oversized chair. She was seated in a normal arm chair. When she stood up, the chair also stood up, sticking firmly to her hips. The crowd was silent, embarrassed for this one they loved so. While two men pulled the chair from Miss Waters, she looked at the crowd and smiled. That was the greatest smile I have ever seen. Three thousand people gave her a standing ovation and she won their hearts.*

Ethel Waters was not only a great actress, she was a very real human being who never forgot her roots, thanking God always for all He had done for her.

Mary C. Crowley, president and founder of Home Interiors in Dallas, was immediately adopted into Ethel's "family" upon meeting. It was love at first sight. Here are Mary's memories of a woman she too called Mom.

I had admired Ethel Waters from afar for many years. In the fall of 1971 I became personally acquainted with her—the beginning of a lifelong friendship.

We were preparing for the Billy Graham Greater Southwest Crusade, which would be the very first function to be held in the Dallas Cowboy Stadium. The committee for the crusade was headed by Coach Tom Landry. It was my privilege to be the only woman to serve on the committee. I was planning a big rally to be held two weeks before the crusade with Ruth Graham as the speaker and Ethel Waters to sing at the rally.

I was so thrilled when I heard that Ruth Graham had accepted, and I chartered a limousine for her and reserved a suite at the Marriott Hotel.

Ethel Waters also was a speaker at that rally. When she arrived, I reserved a limousine for her, too. I had reserved two identical suites of rooms at the hotel for Ruth and Ethel, and sent baskets of flowers to both suites. But when we walked into Ethel's suite, we found it wasn't a suite—it was one room. I simply picked up the phone and insisted the manager find something better—a suite like the one for Ruth.

I didn't think this was much to do, but to Ethel it was a big thing. After that, we continued to correspond. I came to love her for the dedicated Christian that she was.

During the motorcade, as I was riding in the limousine with Ruth and Ethel with the motorcycle escort, I said with excitement, "Oh, this is fun. I've never been in a motorcade with a motorcycle escort before." Ethel, with a deep chuckle added, "Me, too, honey. I have never had one before either."

In 1974, when I was in Los Angeles for a Home Interiors' rally, I called Ethel. She was in low spirits. "My eyes are so bad with these cataracts that I can't see to cook for myself," she said. "But that doesn't matter. I'm not hungry anyway."

"Then I'm coming right out to visit you," I insisted.

"Oh, honey, you can't take time for that. You've got a meeting there with your people," Ethel protested.

"We'll see about that!" I said. I ordered prime ribs with all the fixings from the hotel. Two of my managers drove out with me to her lovely apartment on the fifteenth floor overlooking Los Angeles, and waited two hours for me to visit with Ethel.

Ethel looked so weak and rundown. She could scarcely hold a fork in her hand. As we talked, I helped her eat. I'll never forget that afterward she went and sat by her window overlooking the city that was sparkling with lights. That beautiful, high sweet voice of hers broke out with the Bill and Gloria Gaither song, "I'm going to live the way He wants me to live."

The words of that song still send a thrill up my spine whenever I hear them—and later Ethel was to come to Dallas and sing them at a very special occasion for me and for my family.

How can I ever thank God enough for letting me walk with this spiritual giant?

Kurt Kaiser, vice-president of Word, Inc., as well as an accomplished composer and arranger, had this to say about Ethel:

When I was in the presence of Ethel Waters, I was honored . . . for I was with one of the great artists this country has ever produced. She was smart as a whip, had uncanny insight and her heart reached out to me.

Ethel Waters did not need a rhythm section, for she possessed that wonderful sense of time that few people have. With Reginald Beane at the piano, things absolutely "swung." I will always remember how she totally wrapped herself around a song. When she sang "Mammy," it was out of experience that included glistening cheeks wet with tears. She felt everything very deeply. What she sang deserves many hearings, due to the subtle nuances which were a gift from God.

Our last recording experience, out of which came the album Just a Little Talk with Ethel, was a highlight in my life, and all the people who were associated with me on this project felt a very real sense of history putting the recording together.

I will always feel honored and enriched to have been her friend.

Ernie Chavez, who went beyond the call of duty as a mailman to become a special friend of Ethel's, writes of his loving memories:

I had the privilege of knowing "Mom Waters" who to me was one of the greatest human beings that I have ever met.

She was mean, tough, strong, sweet and very lovable. When she spoke there was always a purpose; therefore, she chose her words very carefully. Sometimes her words were mean and hard, there were also times when she spoke sweet and soft, but her words were always given with an inner love which she possessed very strongly. Life had given her many experiences which made her very wise in all phases of life. She was a woman who had plenty of love and wisdom and was always willing to share it with anyone who was in need of it.

My greatest experience with Ethel's love was when my own mother died. She knew my great loss and sorrow, and she put her arm on my shoulder and said, "Son, I am now your mom." The tenderness of her words and the love pouring out from within gave me a comfort that I will never forget. You see, she really meant it. I knew these weren't just words, for I could feel her love reaching out towards me.

She was some "mom" and I was proud to be her son.

Julie Harris, whose association with Ethel Waters goes back to 1952 when they both played in *The Member of the Wedding* in New York, was a "precious baby girl" of Ethel's. Even though they did not see each other very often, there was a deep mutual love. Julie reminisces of her beloved Ethel:

Oh, how I miss Ethel's presence here. I can always see her— and feel her hands and arms. Her skin was so beautiful and I loved to hold her hands.

Our first meeting was at Robert Whitehead's apartment— Ethel had come there so we could meet and leisurely read the play, The Member of the Wedding. She talked about missing her soap operas on the radio! I loved her immediately. I had seen her in Cabin in the Sky and Mamba's Daughters both in

Detroit and I worshiped her. This was the beginning of our family—Ethel, Brandon DeWilde, Bill Hansen, "Beany" Barker and me.

The year and a half that we did the play was a happy time for me—I belonged—to Ethel, to Brandon. They were the we of me.

"No use complainin'. It only makes the devil happy."

Chapter Nine

"NO-BODY KNOWS THE TROUBLE I see. No-body knows but Jesus." This old Negro spiritual which Ethel had sung many times expressed her feelings. She endured her pain in silence. Time after time I would hear her say when asked how she was feeling, "No use complainin'. It only makes the devil happy."

Ethel had been a fighter since the day she was born. It was obvious she wasn't about to leave this world without a struggle.

With her countless ailments, she often referred to herself as "damaged goods." When a new affliction would arise and I would suggest she see a doctor about it, she would reply, "Oh, no, I just talk to my Heavenly Father about it. He don't take no coffee breaks. He's always there."

Yet she could still smile at herself. "Just call me 'Speedy,'" she commented about her slow walking. "I get tickled at myself sometimes, walking like I had the rickets."

Time after time on my Saturday morning visits, we would each be in our chairs by the window as she would look me in the eye and say, "Twila, I don't know why the Lord doesn't take me home. I've lived a hard life and now I'm weary."

The tears would trickle down her worn cheeks as she would continue, "I'm homesick for heaven."

In my simple way, I would try to convince her she was needed: God had a job yet for her to do.

"I can't let myself get down," she said. "I have to fight to stay on top of things and not let depression set in, or I would never make it. Satan never wants you to be happy. If I stumble and fall, I just get up and say, 'Devil, you're not gonna get me this time.' "

At other times and in better moods she'd say, "I'm sittin on the edge of heaven, and His eye is still on me. I'm not afraid to die, in fact I'm kinda lookin forward to it. I know the Lord has His arms wrapped around this big fat sparrow."

A week after Ethel had sung at the San Diego Billy Graham Crusade in 1976, she called me with her decision to be admitted to a hospital. I knew this decision had not come easy for her.

Her latest affliction—hemorrhaging—was making her extremely weak. On my previous visit with her, she grabbed onto the piano to steady herself as she started to black out. "See, this is what I go through all the time," she told me. I felt so helpless.

Before she had time to change her mind, I had made arrangements for her to enter City of Hope Hospital the next day.

As I arrived at the Bunker Hill Towers to pick her up, she finished packing her bag. Stuffed into a side pocket of her suitcase was her portable radio—she wasn't about to miss her soothing gospel music and her favorite Bible teacher, Dr. Vernon McGee.

I picked up her bag. She took hold of my arm to stabilize herself. "Well, goodbye, little apartment, I'll be back," she said as she glanced around what had been her cozy little home for the past six years.

An hour later we pulled up to the entrance of the hospital.

With the minimum of details, Dr. Ralph Byron's efficient staff had Ethel checked into a private room.

Again, Ethel picked her favorite nurses. The others just couldn't understand how this woman could be so difficult.

Within days the doctors confirmed my suspicion. Ethel had cancer. Because of her age and the condition of her heart, it was too great a risk to operate. Daily radiation treatments were ordered.

On one of my frequent visits to her, I tried not to show my alarm as I noticed the IV's going into her arm, the guard rail on her bed and Ethel lying motionless on her back with the sheets drawn up to her neck. I tried to be cheerful, but I could not get a response from her.

Just then her doctor came into the room, and asked me to step outside while he checked Ethel. On his way out, I stopped him. "What's wrong with her?"

"She doesn't have the will to live," he responded. "Physically, she's no worse than when she came in here."

"Mom, you've got to fight," I told her when I went back in. "You can get better. We need you." Without a movement and in a voice barely audible, she said, "But Twila, you don't know how much pain I'm in."

That hit hard! There was no way I could know what she was going through. Why should she continue fighting? For years now she had longed to meet Jesus face to face.

I left the hospital that day thinking her battle was over. But I had been telling friends for years that she couldn't last long, no one believed me. And, for some unexplainable reason, the fight came back in Ethel. Eventually she gained the strength to walk slowly around her room. The doctors recommended she get some fresh air by taking a ride in a wheel chair. "I'm not about to go outside," she told me as she nixed their idea to get her away from her tiny bleak room.

Ruth Graham, on one of her visits to the West Coast, wanted to see Ethel. I phoned ahead telling Ethel I was bringing a special visitor. Ethel was anxious to see her baby girl, Ruthie, once again. However, our timing was off. Ethel could no longer postpone a trip to the bathroom and our arrival caught Ethel on her way back to bed.

That year as Ruth and Billy sent a Christmas card to Ethel, Ruth added a personal note: "It was so good to see you. Now I've been greeted by choirs, bands, bouquets of flowers, even silence, but never before by a flushing toilet. Leave it up to you to be original."

After Ethel's three-month stay at City of Hope, the doctors felt there was little more they could do for her. The radiation had controlled the cancer. But she was too weak to go back to her apartment alone, and she fought the idea of another convalescent hospital.

"I hate to burden them," Ethel said, "but once Julie and Paul DeKorte said I could stay with them." They had been friends of hers for over fifteen years. Julie was a nurse and could give Ethel the care and attention she needed. "She's a good cook, too," Ethel told me.

I couldn't think of any alternative, even though I knew what a huge responsibility it would be for Julie. But when I called Paul to see if the offer was still good for them to take in Ethel, they readily agreed. A week before Christmas Julie drove Ethel to their home in a borrowed camper (Ethel refused to leave by ambulance and wasn't able to sit up in a car.) Paul's study had been cleared and a rented hospital bed was set up. A Christmas tree was in the corner.

As the months rolled by, that little corner of the DeKortes' home became home to Ethel. Slowly their oil paintings came down and pictures of Ethel went up.

Ethel's recovery was slow. If she got out of bed, it was only to take a few steps to the bathroom. Only once during her entire stay at the DeKorte's did she venture out of her room. Christmas morning she slowly made her way to the family room. While the DeKorte family was having their breakfast

Ethel softly began to sing, "I just want to thank the Lord." From the bottom of her heart she was truly thankful to be spending Christmas with a loving, caring Christian family.

It seemed doubtful that Ethel would ever be able to return to her "little nest" at Bunker Hill Towers. Yet she refused to give it up. To her it represented security, a place to call her own.

I was saving money for a study tour to Russia when my boss came up with the idea of subleasing my apartment and moving into Ethel's rent free. Even though Ethel and I were close, I was too timid to ask her for favors. Bill Brown presented the idea to her and she responded, "Why didn't you think of that months ago?" She was glad for another opportunity where she could be of help to me.

I was excited about moving into the swanky Bunker Hill Towers and was especially thrilled with the facilities it offered—tennis courts, Jacuzzi, sauna and gym.

Before I could move in, some of Ethel's things had to come out. Julie and I packed her belongings.

We soon discovered Ethel saved everything—and I mean everything. "Do you think she'd miss this?" Julie and I would question each other. Yet we were scared to throw anything away. Ethel knew exactly everything she owned and where it was kept.

Julie and I laughed when we came upon tiny pieces of soap Ethel had collected in a plastic bag. Why would she want to keep these? It seemed useless to pack the bag so we agreed to toss it out. One of the first things Ethel asked was if we had found her Castile soap. They were keepsakes from World War II!

One of the things Ethel especially asked Julie to pack and bring to her room were her old classic records. She had told Julie, "I know Twila likes to entertain and the records are something her friends might walk out with." She trusted me but not my friends . . . !

That Saturday we loaded up the DeKortes' station wagon until there was barely room for the driver. Yet we had hardly made a dent in Ethel's possessions. The closets were jammed with clothes and shoes, though she only wore three or four favorites. Dresser drawers were full with scarfs, purses, and bed linen still in the plastic wrappers. The kitchen was equipped with every gadget imaginable.

I moved my necessities into apartment #1502. Gradually we moved Ethel's belongings to the DeKortes. I enjoyed two and a half months of leisure living, yet to me it was always Ethel's place and I was just the visitor.

One typical Friday evening at home, I settled on the adjust-a-bed and turned on the remote control TV to watch the local news. The ding dong of the phone interrupted my quietness. It was Ernie, Ethel's mailman. He had just learned that Ethel had been taken suddenly to the Westpark Hospital. I called Paul who gave me the details of how to get to the hospital.

It was "stop and go" on the freeway to the hospital. I prayed, "Oh Lord, please let me see Mom one more time. Please keep her alive until I get there." I felt guilty I hadn't been to see her too often in Chatsworth. Knowing she had Julie to care for her, the responsibility did not weigh so heavily on me.

It took an hour to reach the hospital. The receptionist told me Ethel was in intensive care. I hurried through the maze of corridors to the ICU. One of the nurses told me to have a seat and Julie would be out soon. The moment she came through the swinging doors she assured me everything was okay. It wasn't a heart attack. I was relieved that it wasn't as serious as it seemed.

Julie explained to me that Ethel had passed out and the paramedics were immediately called to revive her with oxygen. Ethel despised hospitals but agreed to go when one of the paramedics said, "She won't live through the night if we don't get her to a hospital." Her instinct of survival was strong. Within two days she was back at the DeKorte's home with her own oxygen tank nearby.

As Mother's Day approached, I made plans to spend the day with Ethel. This would give Julie a chance to get away without worrying.

Two days before, however, Ethel was admitted to the West Hills Hospital. This time it was blood clots in her right leg.

I drove the twenty-five miles in the pouring rain to spend the afternoon with Mom. I was there only a few minutes when she turned to me and said, "Well, kiddo, I don't want to hold you up." That was always my cue she was ready for me to leave.

Before I left Ethel said, "I'm running a close race with Job." But like him, she was not about to give in to the devil.

Ethel never quit being an actress, even in days of suffering. Bill Brown and Cliff Barrows spent several hours with her one afternoon at the DeKortes' home. She had them convinced her health was improving and she was going to sing at one more crusade. They wondered why I had told them she really was in such bad condition. However, what they didn't know was that she used up every ounce of strength talking with them. Immediately after they left, Julie had to give her oxygen, the penalty for overexuberance.

I teased Ethel I could write a book about the conditions and facilities of various hospitals in the Los Angeles area—I had visited so many. Her next trip was to the Motion Picture Country Hospital in Woodland Hills. Gangrene had started in her foot, causing it to swell and turning her toes black. She would wince in pain with every attempted step. Yet there was nothing the doctors could do but keep a close check on it as it gradually began to deteriorate. It was too great a risk to amputate.

According to Ethel, hospital food was always cold or not

seasoned right. The nurses kept coming into the room whether you needed them or not. The doctor's probing only made her more uncomfortable. The repeated questioning, "How are you doing today?" by the cheerful staff was almost too much for her. No matter how hard they all tried, they couldn't please her.

Julie did all she could to ease Ethel's worrying. She would cook bacon at home and take it to Ethel for her breakfast. Every day she would stop by to visit. Several nights she slept on a cot in the hospital room, knowing her presence soothed Ethel's frustrations.

One of the few things that seemed to help her frazzled nerves was hearing God's word on her portable radio and talking to Him moment by moment.

"I don't understand it," Ethel would softly say, "I don't know why I have to suffer so." Yet she never blamed God for all her pain and agony. She only praised Him for being so good to her.

On one visit I recall she wanted to know if I had time to sit down and listen to a cassette recording of her which was made in 1954. Her old friend, Reggie Beane, had brought it from New York. I sat down and started the cassette hearing such tunes as "I Ain't Gonna Sin No More," "Half of Me," and "Bread and Gravy." She didn't have the strength to sing aloud but her lips formed each word and I marveled that she remembered every lyric. Occasionally she would wince in pain, but for forty-five minutes her own music from her one-woman show brightened her world.

Ethel refused to let the doctors increase her pain medicine. She was afraid of being "hooked" on drugs. Finally, when the pain became unbearable, she decided to risk surgery and have a colostomy. What did she have to lose? If she survived, the pain would lessen and if she died she would be completely out of pain.

The surgery was scheduled, and presurgery tests were

begun when the doctors discovered Ethel's kidneys were failing. Surgery was now out of the question.

Ethel was becoming more and more miserable at the Motion Picture Hospital. We knew she would not be happy in any hospital, but Julie arranged for her to return to the Westpark Hosital, hoping her attitude would improve.

There, the doctors ordered a catheter for Ethel which immediately brought relief. Therefore, she refused to continue with her pain pills. But even though her dosage had not been strong, she still experienced withdrawal symptoms. Ethel couldn't understand her emotional turbulence. She had her highs and lows and even hallucinations.

One Saturday as I walked to her bedside, she tightly grasped my hand and said, "Please, Twila, please, promise me you won't betray me. The people around here think I'm losing my mind. Tell me I'm not going crazy." I quietly assured her she was very sane and that I would do whatever I could to help her. She could count on me.

After several more weeks in the hospital, the doctors felt there was nothing more they could do. Ethel knew it wouldn't be long before she would be in heaven, and therefore she pleaded with Julie to take her home. "I want to die in my own bed," she said.

It was not an easy task for Julie to care for the bed-ridden patient, but she was determined to make Ethel's last days as happy as possible. Ethel was moved by ambulance back to the DeKortes'.

Her room was equipped with the necessities—the overhead bar to help her lift herself, the portable potty, the hospital scales, the bed tray, and the oxygen tanks in the corner to help her breathe and which she used around the clock. The pretty blue sheets and the hand-made quilt from the sisters at St. Theresa's monastery (a charity Ethel had given to for many years) perked up the room so it didn't look so much like a hospital.

Ethel continued to get weaker and it became increasingly difficult for her to talk.

Her left arm and leg were swollen because of poor circulation, and her foot was black from the gangrene. She was regularly taking her pain pills again. It hurt to see her like that. Her pride prohibited her from allowing many visitors. I knew each day was so long for her as she lay on her back. It was even difficult for her to roll over to reach her phone on the stand beside the bed. Her only contact with the outside world was her color TV and the radio, as she kept up on the news events of each day.

A few months before she had told me to watch her movie, The Sound and the Fury, on the late show. I was not sorry I missed my sleep as I viewed this woman of over three hundred pounds running freely around the house and yard as she played the maid. It was hard to imagine her as the same woman now so helpless.

Ethel didn't like evening visitors, so I was limited to seeing her on Saturdays and Sundays. As I left on August 27, I tenderly kissed her on the forehead and said, "Well, I'll see you next Saturday."

"Maybe," she weakly said, "just maybe." I immediately wondered if that were a premonition.

The following Tuesday Julie called me at work and I volunteered to help by spending the night at the DeKortes'. Ethel was getting much weaker, and it was impossible for Julie to lift her. "I'll be glad to do what I can to help," I told Julie. "I would never make it as a nurse. I don't have the stamina to do what you do."

That night we propped Ethel up on the edge of the bed. Her back ached from lying still all day long. I gently began to massage it. I was amazed at how bony her shoulders were. Her thin white hair was fluffed around her face as she dropped her head and said, "O, dear Jesus, how much longer?"

146

I struggled to conceal my feelings. I didn't want Ethel to see how difficult this was for me.

I rubbed her swollen leg which seemed to ease the pain momentarily. We helped her lie back down and tucked the sheets around her.

Julie picked up Ethel's Bible which had been given to her by the Billy Graham Team. It automatically opened to Psalm 71, Ethel's comfort in this time of trouble, as it had been many times before. It was underlined in pencil.

Julie and I perched on each side of the bed as Julie began to read:

In thee, O Lord, do I put my trust: let me never be put to confusion. . . . I am as a wonder unto many; but thou art my strong refuge. Let my mouth be filled with thy praise and with thy honour all the day. Cast me not off in the time of old age; forsake me not when my strength faileth. . . . . . . Now also when I am old and greyheaded, O God, forsake me not; until I have shewed thy strength unto this generation, and thy power to every one that is to come. . . .

Then Julie prayed for God's wisdom and comfort during this difficult time. After the *Amen*, Ethel weakly turned to me and said, "Wasn't that a sweet prayer?"

Julie spent that night sleeping in the recliner chair in Ethel's room. The past few nights she had been sleeping on the living room sofa to be near Ethel. Even the sofa was too far away that night.

The next morning I again helped Julie sit Ethel up on the edge of the bed and rubbed her back. I kissed her goodbye as I left for my office. I felt so helpless.

How much more could this woman take?

"I'll be looking for you in Heaven."

Chapter Ten

"TWILA...SHE'S GONE," the tear-choked voice said over the other end of the phone.

My intuition had told me that the early morning call that first day of September was Julie. "Oh, no," I reacted. I knew it was coming yet I wasn't totally prepared for that statement.

"Did she go easy?" I asked Julie as the realization pierced my mind. "Yes," Julie softly replied, "I wish you could see her peaceful look now."

Julie had spent that night, as she had the last few, in the chair at the foot of the bed. At 4:30 A.M. she was awakened and moved to Ethel's side. Ethel opened her eyes and feebly murmured her last words, "I love you." Then all was quiet. At 6:30 A.M. Julie again was awakened by gasps. An hour later Ethel's heart stopped.

I was numb as Julie said to me, "Have a good cry and when you get to your office, give me a call."

What do I do now? Where do I begin? My mind was racing with thoughts and questions.

I made it to my office in a daze and called Julie. The next

step was to notify friends before they heard it on the news. It was decided I should go to Forest Lawn to make the necessary arrangements for the funeral and burial.

As I sat in the Forest Lawn reception room, I couldn't help remembering one of the times Ethel told me how anxious she was to go to heaven.

"When I get there," she said, "I'm gonna say, 'Hey, you over there, move over. And you up front, sit down. I wanna get a better look at my Jesus.'" I imagine it only took moments for her to race past St. Peter to get to her Master's side. In my mind I could see her throwing those big brown loving arms around Jesus and saying, "I'm finally home." I could visualize her sitting at Jesus' feet saying "I love you so much, Jesus. You were so good to me," as she forgot about all the suffering and hardship she had endured on earth.

I awoke from my mental dreaming as the counselor came into the room. He had been a fan of Ethel's, he told me. Then we were down to business.

Since it was Labor Day weekend, did we want to wait until Tuesday for the service? What time? Who would be the minister? Who would sing? What songs? Had we picked out a casket? What type of vault? Did we want the service to be private? How many memory folders? My mind was whirling as I made decision after decision. Then I had to talk to the florist and the cosmetologist.

Two and a half hours later I was back in my office to the sound of ringing phones. The press had been alerted and were calling to confirm the fact, friends were calling to extend sympathy and offer help, and there were still many decisions to be made. Somehow the day went whirling by.

As I watched the TV news that night, I was awed by the beautiful tributes the stations carried about Ethel. However, I was upset that they were saying she died in poverty. That absolutely wasn't true. I had taken care of her checkbook for years and knew she wasn't penniless. The Billy Graham Association faithfully supported her, and she had tucked away royalty checks in savings accounts. She too used to get upset at reports that she was broke. "People think I'm living in a hut and holdin' a tin cup—it's not true."

Not only was my phone busy at the office but it rang at home too. Long-lost friends and relatives Ethel undoubtedly didn't know she had were crawling "out of the woodwork." Where had they been when Ethel needed them?

I was so caught up in the details of planning the funeral that it wasn't until days later that I realized how much I was going to miss her. The person I had loved for over seven years and one who had loved me in return was no longer there to give or accept my love. I once had told Ethel, "I need you and you need me." That's why we had such a beautiful relationship. Now a channel of love was missing from my life.

On September 6, the pieces all came together for the service. I left my office early for Forest Lawn to check on last minute details. There I found Dr. Grady Wilson readying his message. He had flown in that morning from Jackson, Mississippi, where he was holding an evangelistic crusade. I went over with him the order of service that Julie and I had planned.

The mahogany casket was in place in the front of the Church of the Recessional. It was closed but surrounded by flowers sent from Sammy Davis, Jr., Pearl Bailey, Irving Berlin, MGM Studios, as well as the Billy Graham Team and a host of other friends. I checked the casket arrangements which I had ordered—purple mums, lavender roses and white carnations. The ribbon said "MOM."

At 1:30 P.M. I took my place in the front pew with Sue MacDonald, an old friend of Ethel's who had come from Philadelphia, Reginald Beane, Ethel's accompanist for over forty years, and Mary Crowley, Ethel's dear friend from Dallas.

Ethel's precious son, as she called Dr. Grady Wilson of the Billy Graham Association, began the service.

"Ethel Waters has been homesick—but now she's home."

Wow, he's so right, I thought to myself. Time and time again she told me how she looked forward to going to heaven.

Dr. Wilson continued the service reading the entire 71st Psalm. I was so glad God honored her prayer of that first verse to "never be put to confusion." Even at age eighty, her mind was sharp to the end.

Dr. Wilson prayed: "Thank you Father and God for this glorious homegoing of our long-time friend and Thy faithful anointed servant whose life and witness and songs have thrilled millions of people throughout the entire world. We pray that Thou wouldst comfort hearts now of loved ones and friends and neighbors."

I tried to be brave. The service was really a happy occasion for me, because I knew Ethel was no longer in pain. My tears were selfish ones as I realized how much I would miss her.

Dick Bolks and Paul DeKorte sang one of Ethel's favorite songs, "Just a Closer Walk with Thee." I visualized her singing that song to the crusade audience. Her face would glow, her eyes would sparkle and she would have that big Waters grin. The laughs, the tears and the fun we shared at crusades were now just happy memories.

George Beverly Shea sang another of Ethel's favorites—"What a Friend We Have in Jesus." I remembered that just a few days ago when I visited her and that song came on her radio, she had tried to muster enough strength to sing along. Jesus truly was her best friend.

Billy and Ruth Graham were overseas when they learned of Ethel's death. Since Mr. Graham was on his way to preach behind the Iron Curtain, they could not be a part of the service. However, he sent the following telegram which Dr. Wilson read at the service:

I am sending this from Austria on my way to Hungary. Ethel Waters was one of the most unforgettable characters I ever knew. She was a superstar not only on stage and screen but in her personal religious faith. Born in poverty she rose to this height. Though she was world famous she was humble, gracious and generous. After her rededication to Christ in 1957 she became a member of our team and one of our closest friends and counselors. Her good common sense and deep spiritual commitment caused hundreds to seek her advice and counsel on many subjects. In her own way she did as much for race relations as any American in the 20th Century. The last time I saw her she was looking forward with great anticipation to going to heaven. Our loss has been heaven's gain.

Dr. Wilson related a story of several years ago. Ethel was joining his evangelistic campaign in Washington County in the State of Maine. It was in the middle of winter and the deep snows had fallen. An airline stewardess recognized her and said, "Miss Waters, what on earth are you doing way up here in Maine this cold time of the year?" Very quickly Ethel replied, "I'm on my way to a crusade for Christ." The stewardess responded, "Well, for heaven's sake."

Ethel quipped, "That's right, baby. It's for heaven's sake,"

Dr. Wilson continued, "Everything she has done for these past twenty years has been for heaven's sake. She has been a messenger of communication.

"The press has reported she died in poverty. Ladies and gentlemen, that's a terrible mistake. She was fabulously rich in heaven's treasures. Years ago she believed what her Savior said about laying up for yourself 'treasures in heaven where neither moth nor rust doth corrupt and thieves cannot break through and steal.'

"This day we celebrate Ethel Waters's homegoing. What a radiant saint of God she was! She was such a blessing to all wherever she went."

I thought of the time after the 1971 big earthquake in Los Angeles and I called Ethel to see if she were all right. "Oh, honey, I'm okay," she said. "I wasn't afraid. I just said, 'Jesus, you've got my address and I've got yours. Just let me know what you want.'"

By tape recording Ethel Waters once again had the last words:

> So why should I feel discouraged,
> Why should the shadows come,
> Why should my heart be lonely
> Away from heaven and home,
> When Jesus is my portion?
> My constant friend is He:
> His eye is on the sparrow.
> And I know He watches me.
> His eye is on the sparrow,
> And I know He watches me.
>
> I sing because I'm happy,
> I sing because I'm free.
> For His eye is on the sparrow
> And I know He watches me.

After the benediction, the more than one hundred people including Pearl Bailey, John T. Bubbles, Ethel's old vaudeville friend, as well as members of the cast of *The Member of the Wedding* filed past the casket.

The casket-carriers lifted the beautiful wooden box into the hearse. The procession began winding down the road of the Forest Lawn Memorial Park.

We had asked three of Ethel's dearest friends to give eulogies at the graveside. Mary Crowley recalled her memories of Ethel sitting by her apartment window singing along with a Bill Gaither album.

> There's been time when giving
> and loving brought pain.
> and I promised
> I would never let it happen again:
> but I found out that loving
> was well worth the risk,
> and that even in losing you win.
>
> I'm going to live the way He wants me to live,
> I'm going to give until there's just no more to give;
> I'm going to love, love 'til there's just no more love
> I could never outlove the Lord!

Those words perfectly described our Mom.

Cy Jackson, a friend of twenty years, told of the joys of knowing this great woman. He ended his eulogy by quoting Leonard Feather who had written in the *Los Angeles Times*: "She was beautiful in her youth, dignified in middle age, poignant in her final years. She will be long remembered by those of us for whom, at some point in our lives, happiness was just a woman called Ethel."

Reginald Beane concluded the eulogies by telling about "LaBelle," his nickname for Ethel. He then read a poem they both had loved.

The sky was a vivid blue above the tree tops. The bright sunshine pushed the temperature into the 90s as we concluded our celebration of Ethel's homegoing. A bundle of memories flooded my mind as I stood at the graveside of my other Mom.

In particular, I remembered a telegram I had sent for her to Vincente Minnelli, the director of the film *Cabin in the*

Sky, when she was unable to attend a special dinner for him. It said: "It grieves me not to be able to physically attend your wonderfully deserved affair. As you know, due to my confinement, I will be there in spirit. A long time has passed since *Cabin*, although Petunia has always valued your love and friendship. I want to personally invite you and each in attendance to visit me in my 'Cabin in the Sky.' "

That was Ethel's invitation to everyone she met. If she were here to help me end this book, she would say, "Tell them Ethel says, 'I'll be looking for you in heaven.' "